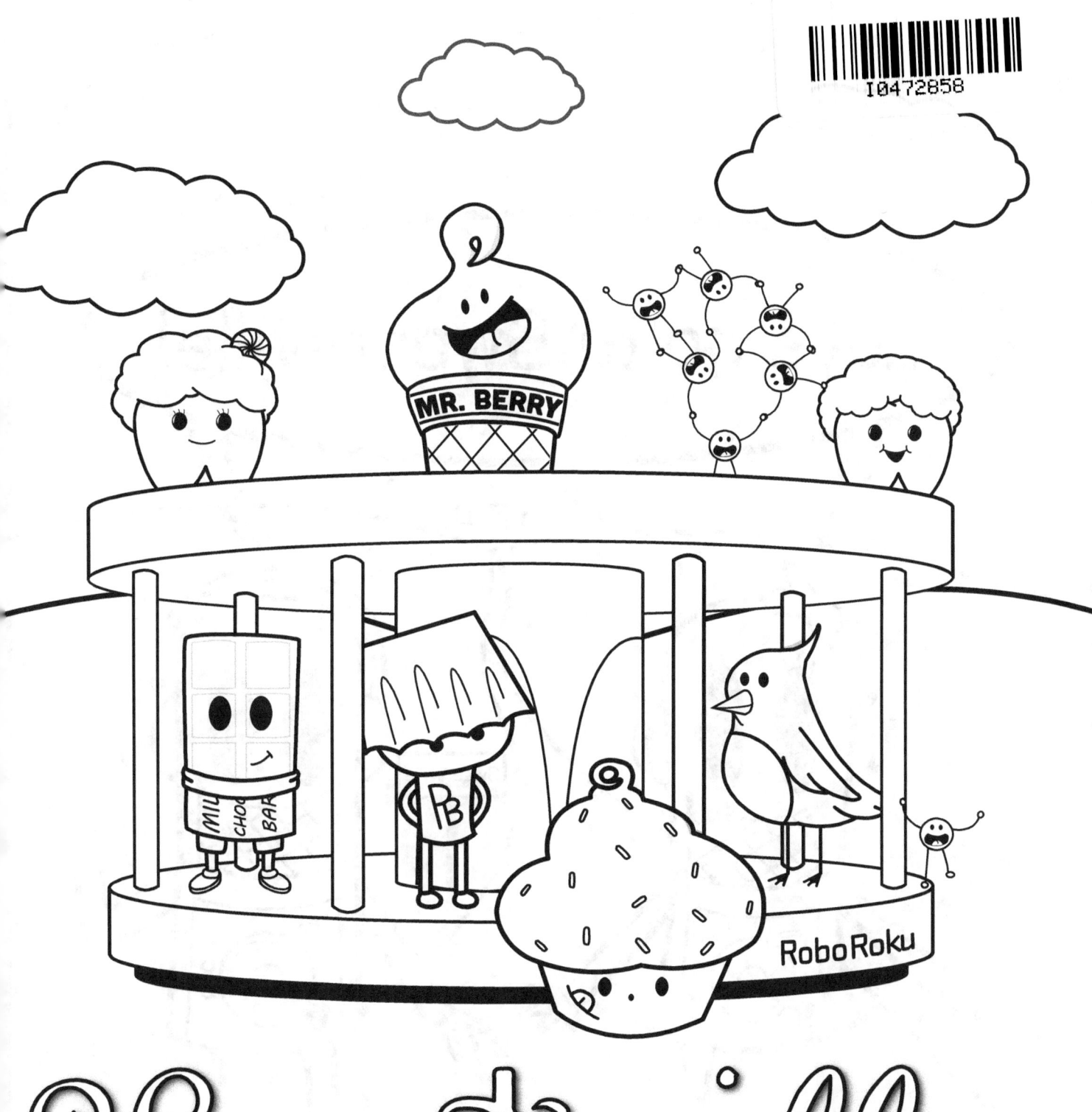

Sweetsville

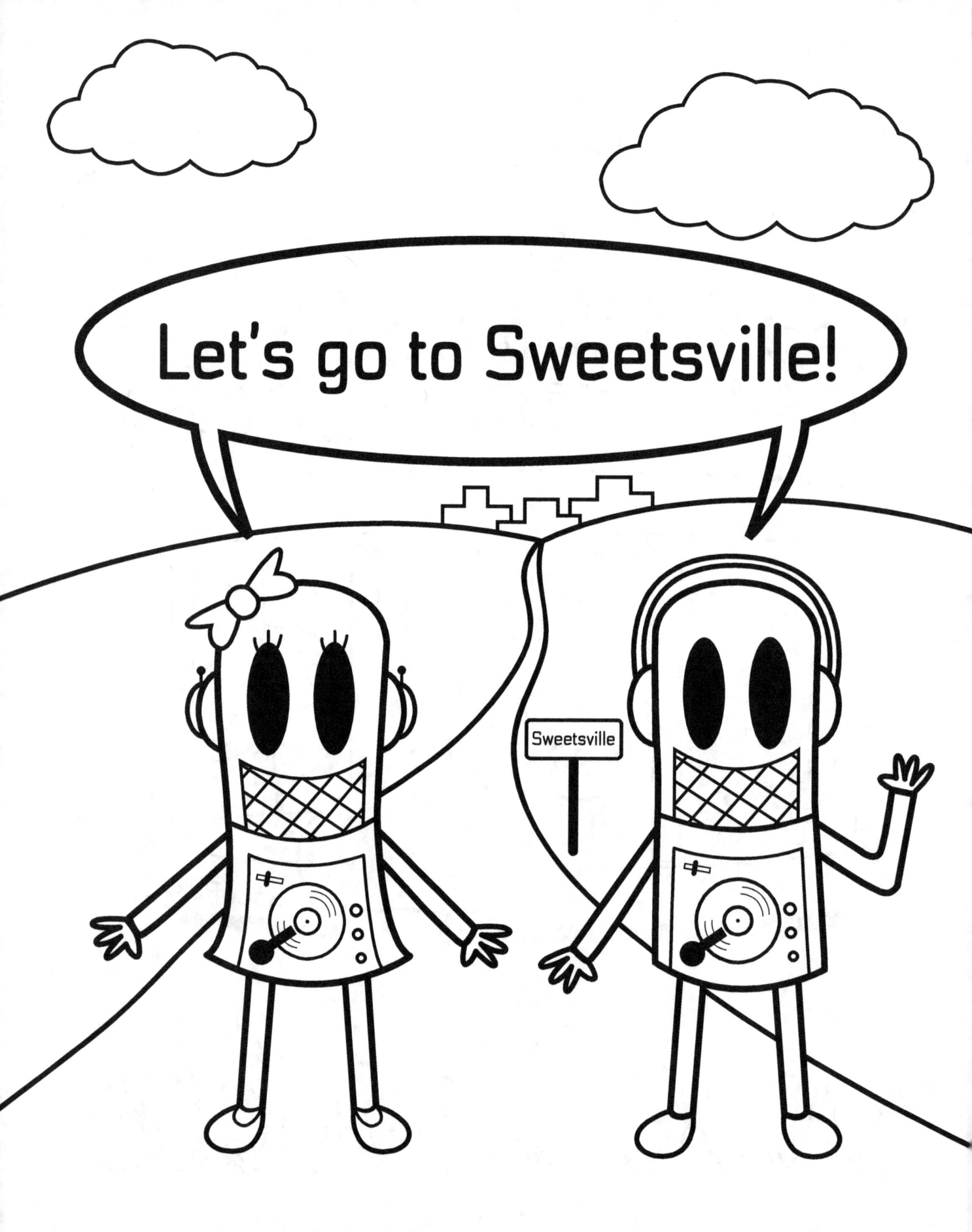

Who lives in Sweetsville? Let's meet the residents!

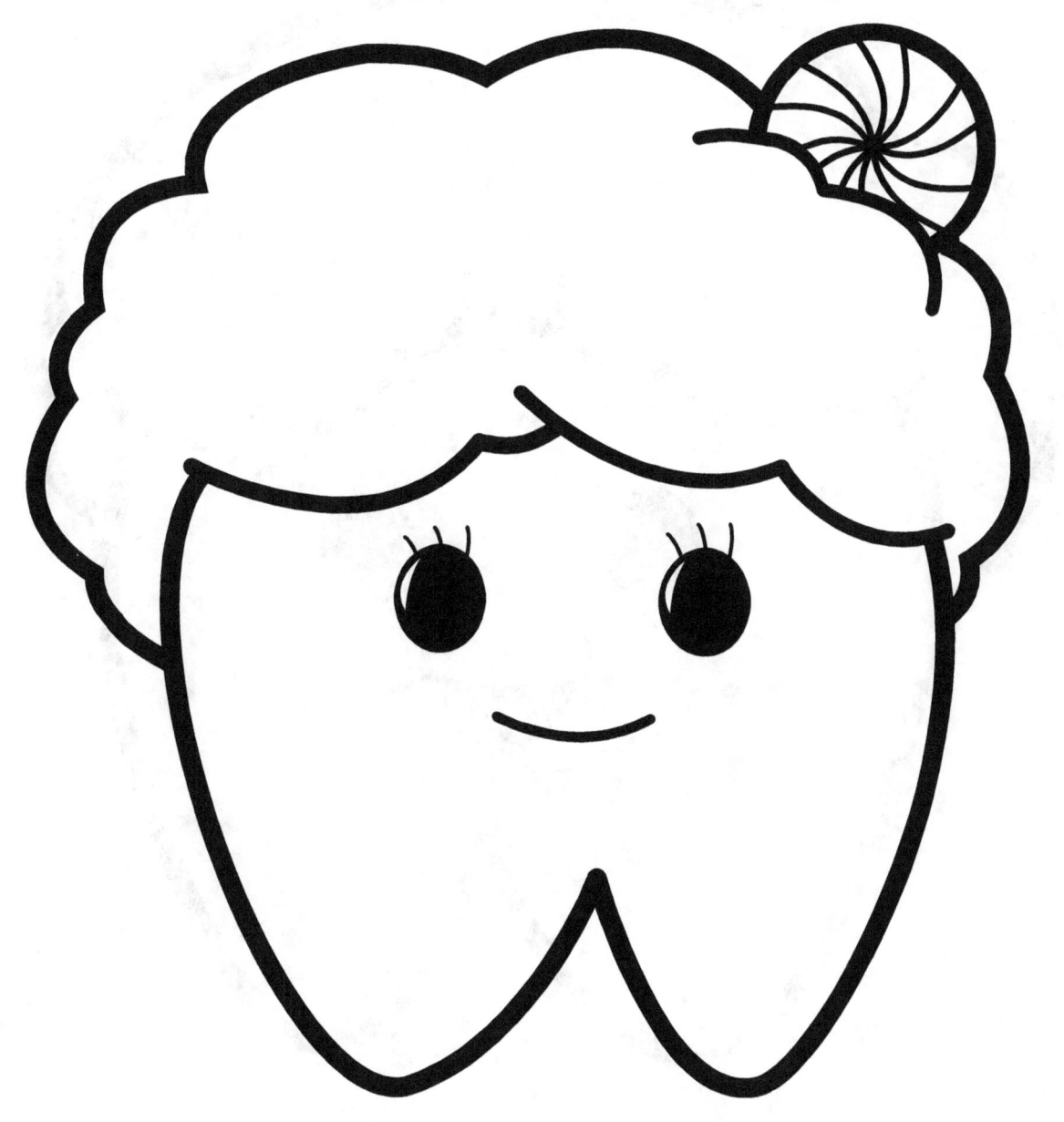

Sweetie Tooth

Sweetie Tooth has a brother.

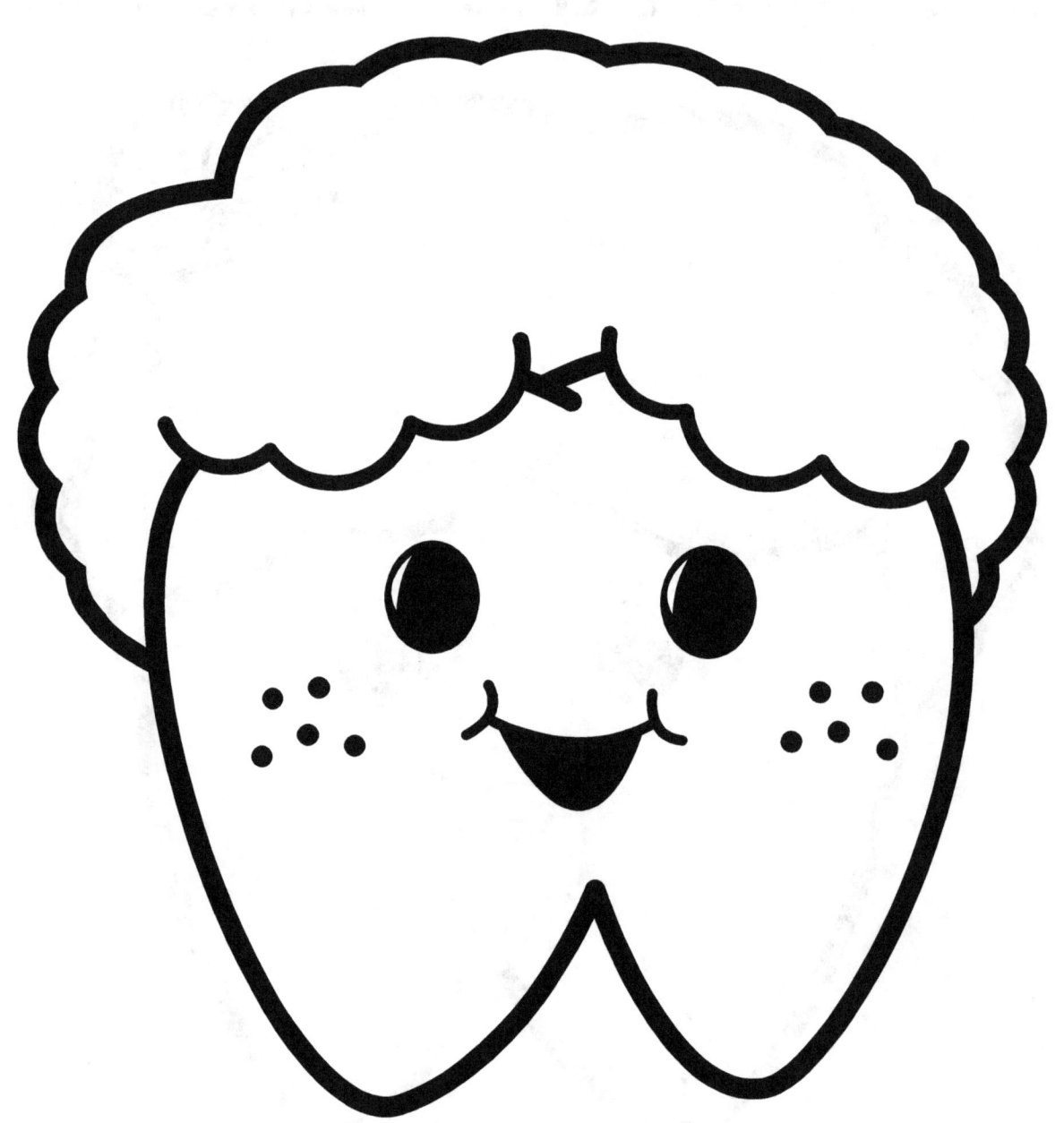

His name is Gingervitis!

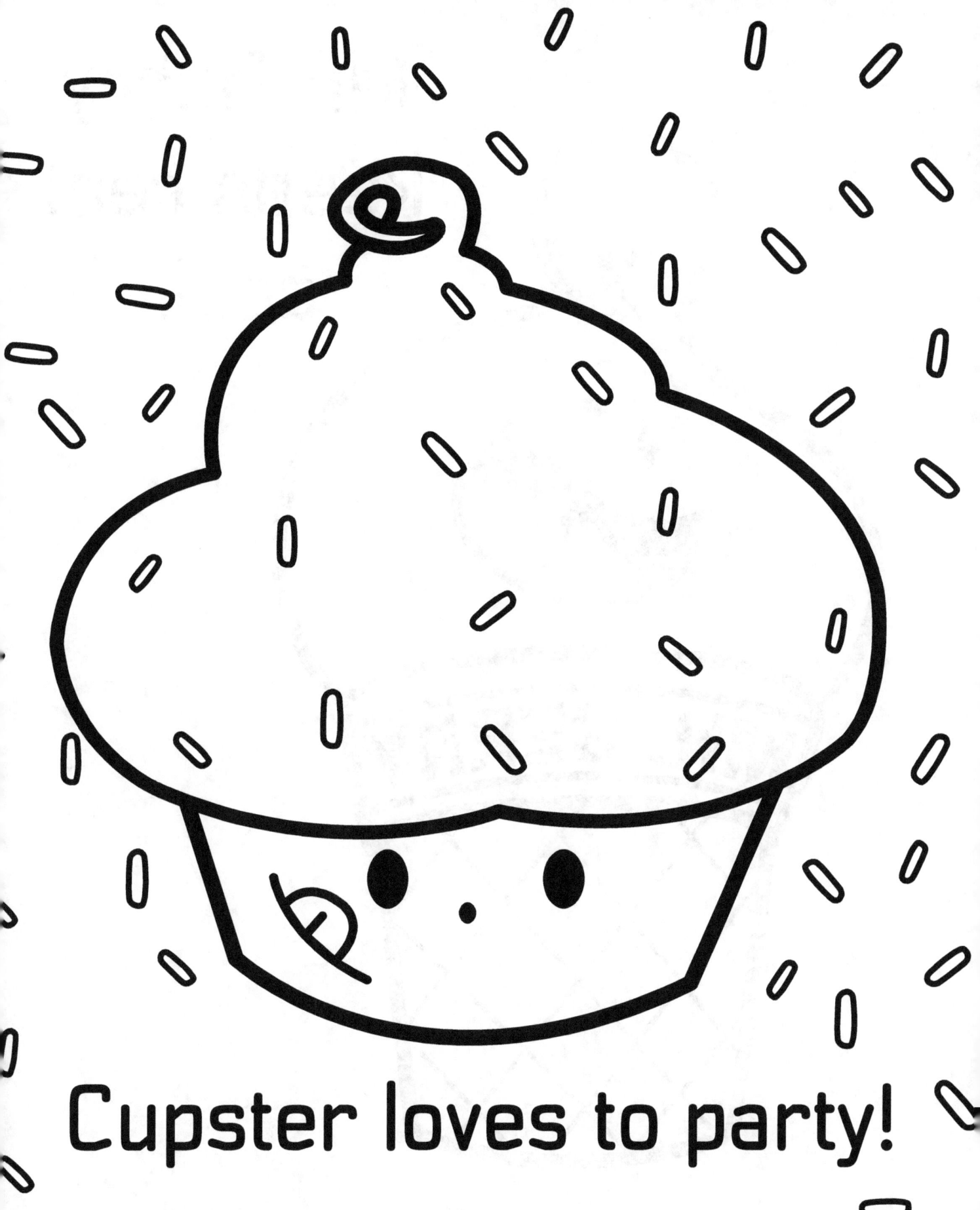

Cupster loves to party!

Mr. Berry
keeps real
cool.

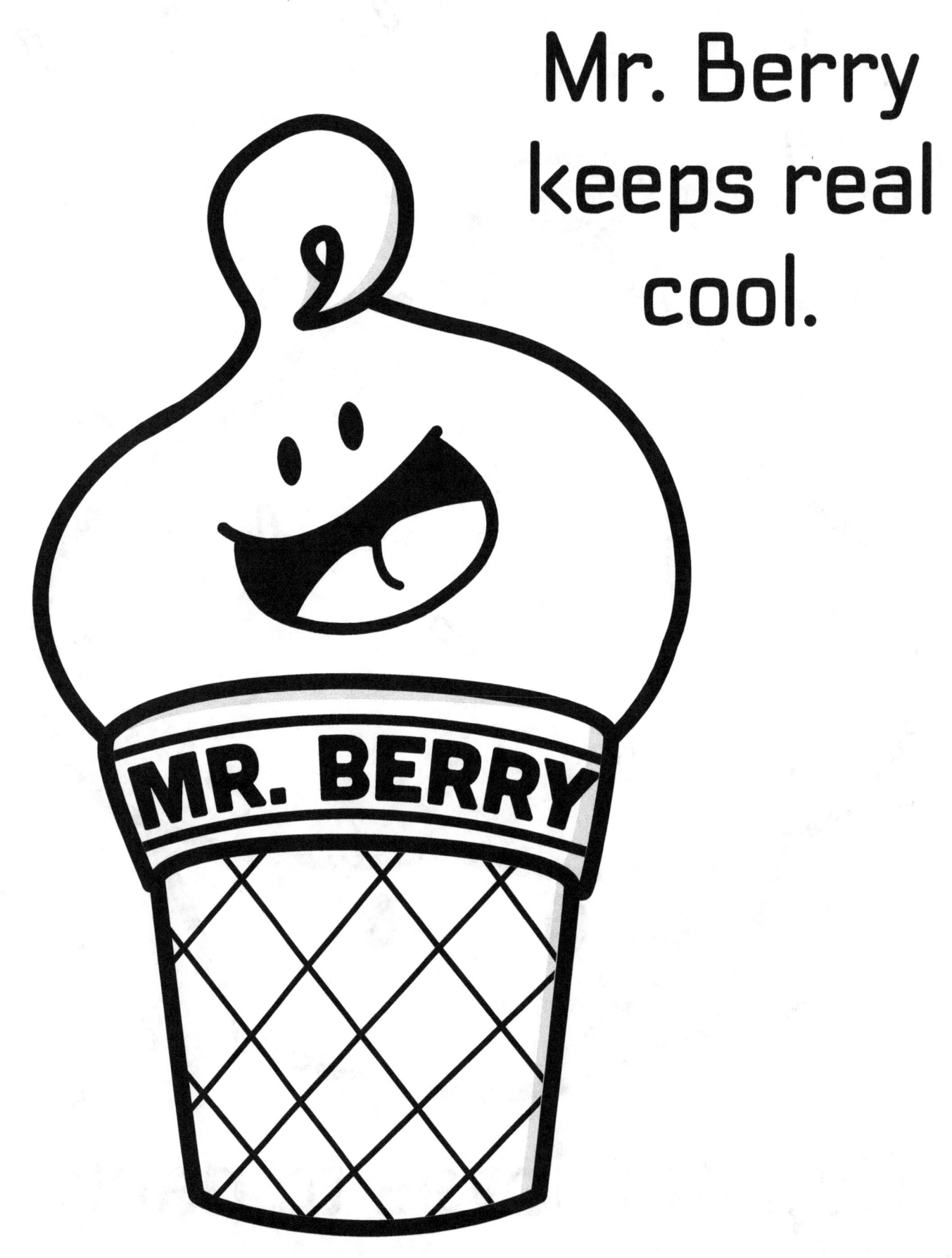

Mike Chocolate is as sweet as can be.

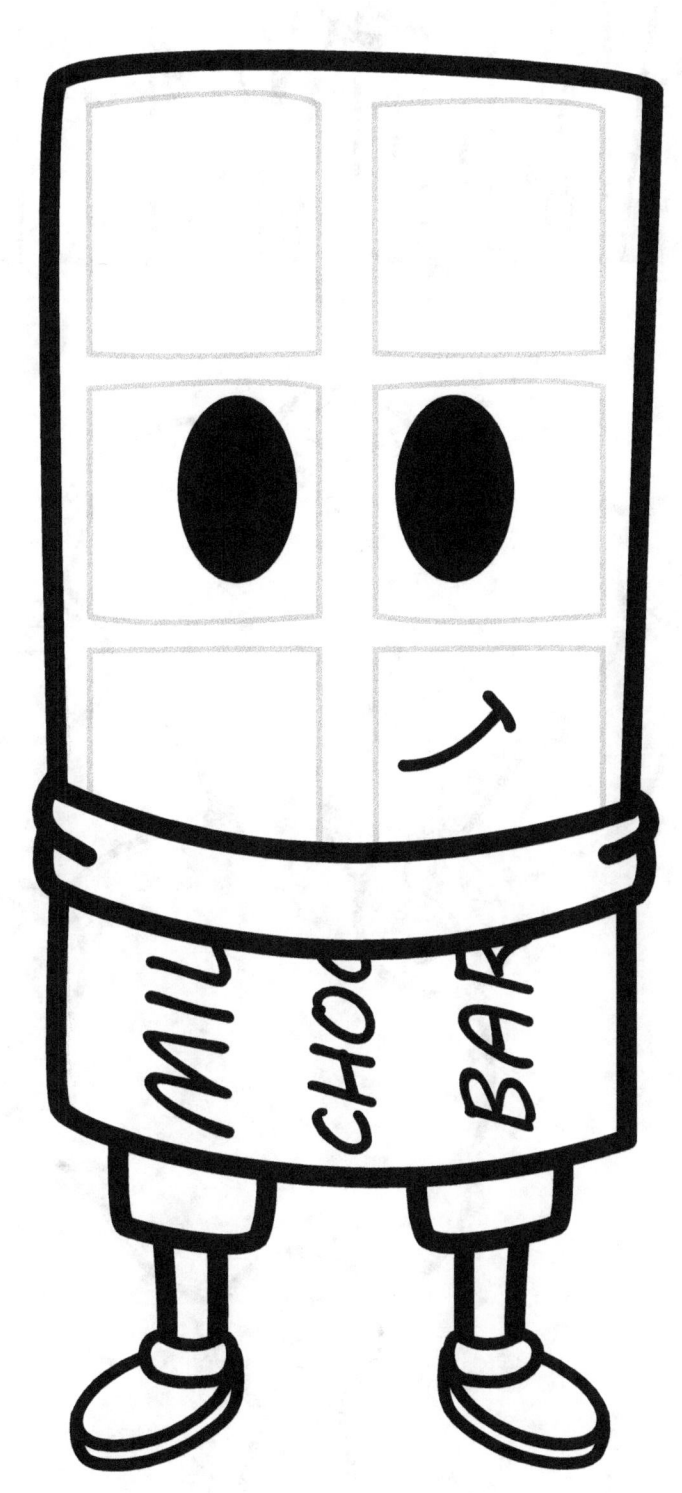

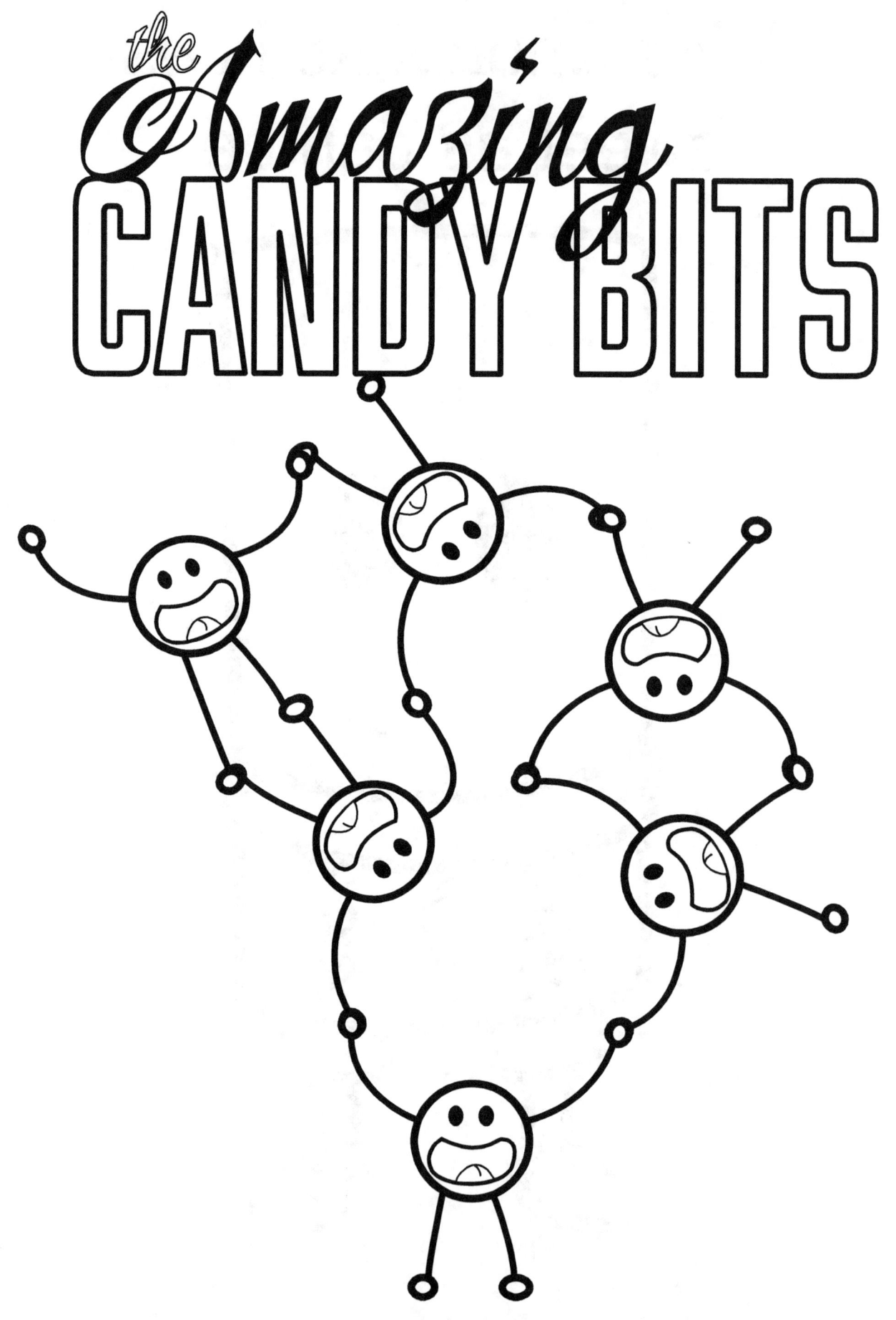

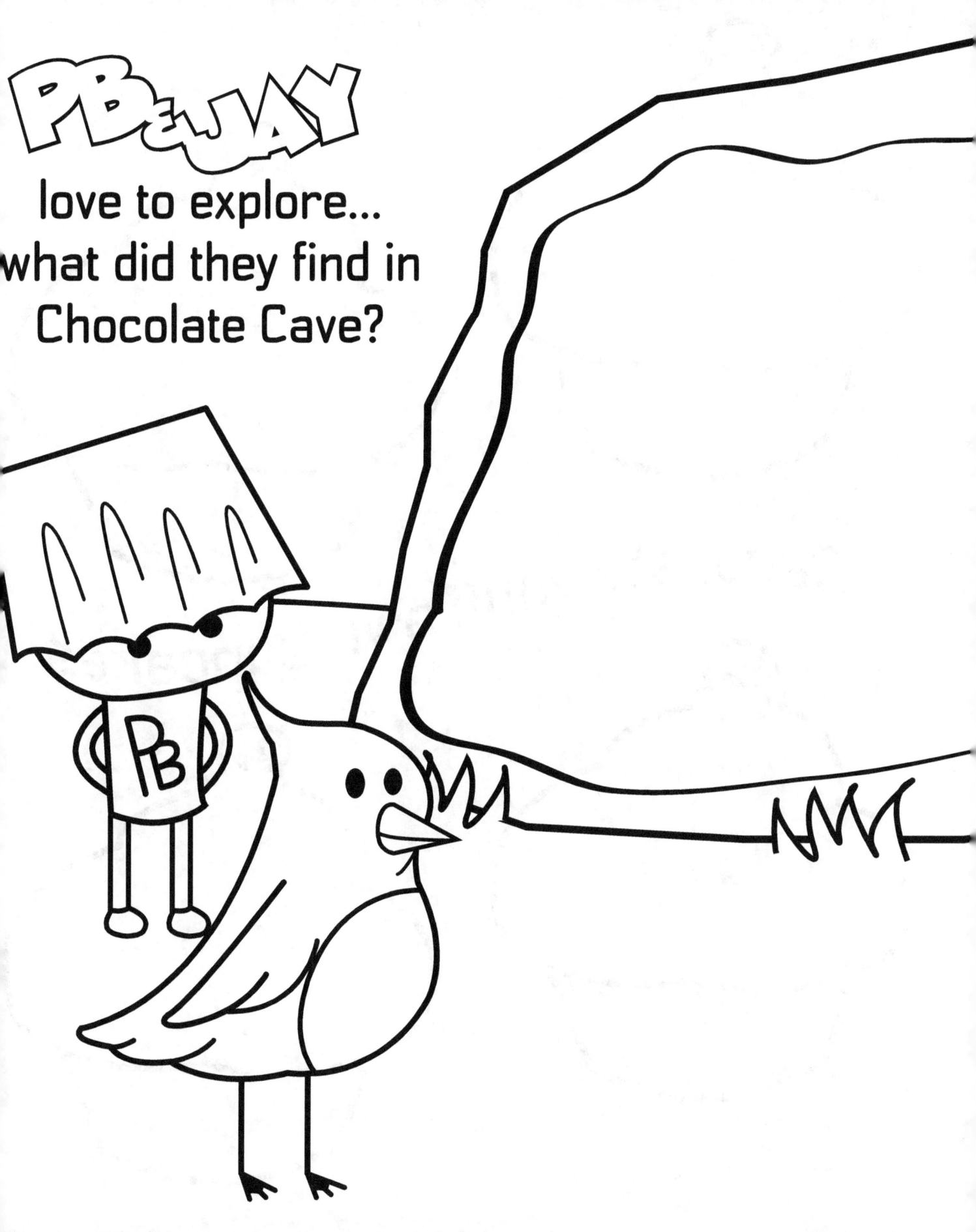

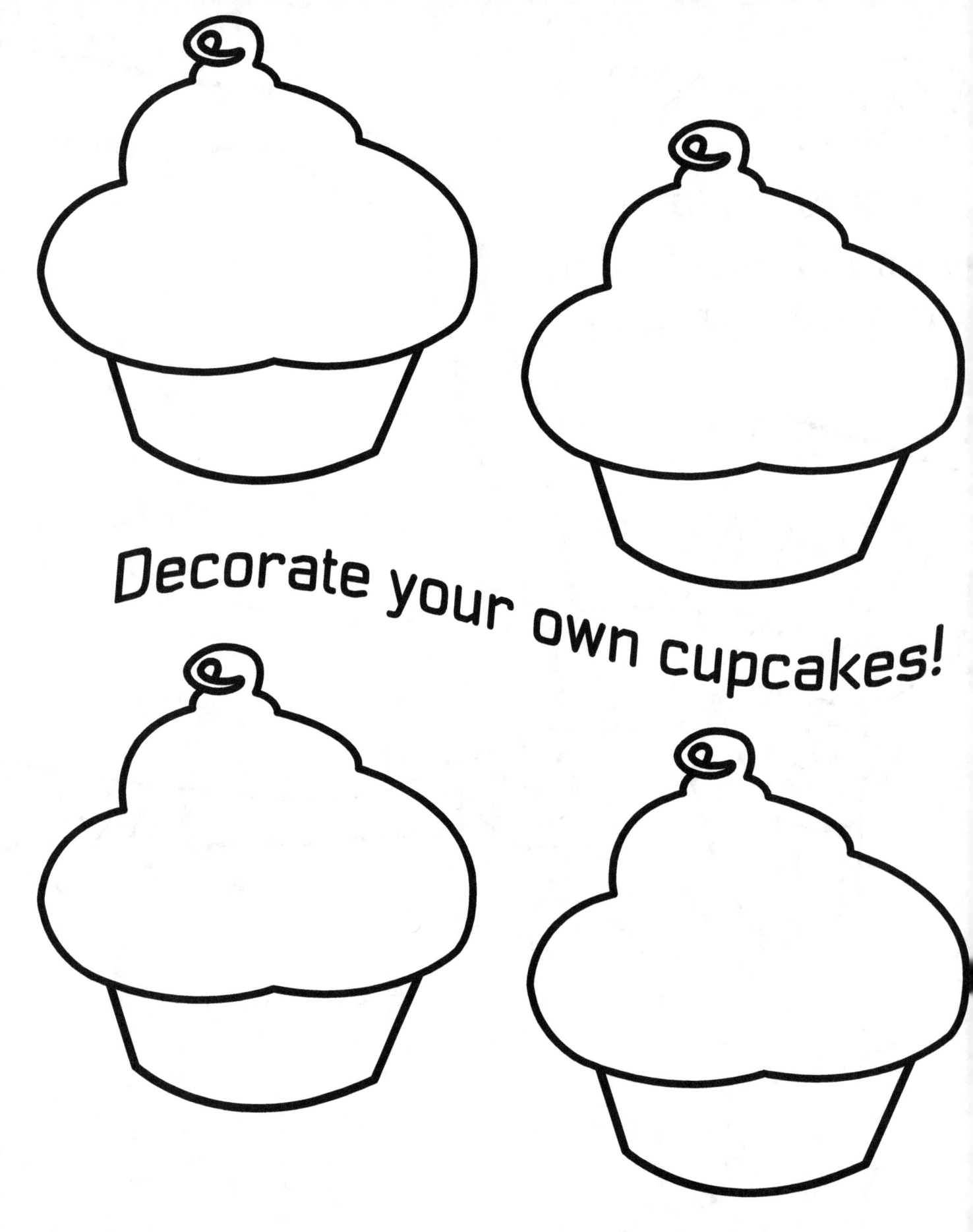

Decorate your own cupcakes!

LET'S GO CAMPING!

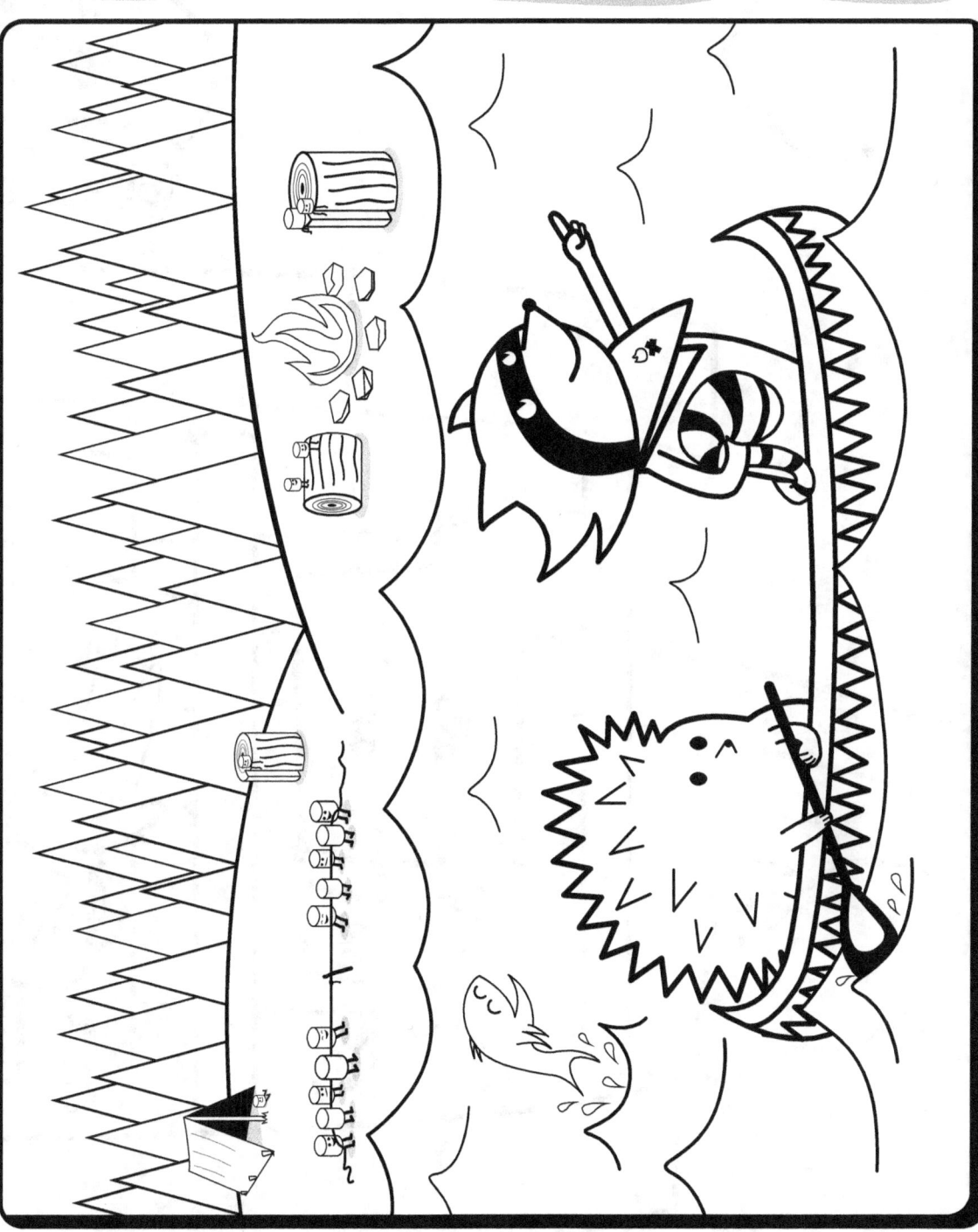

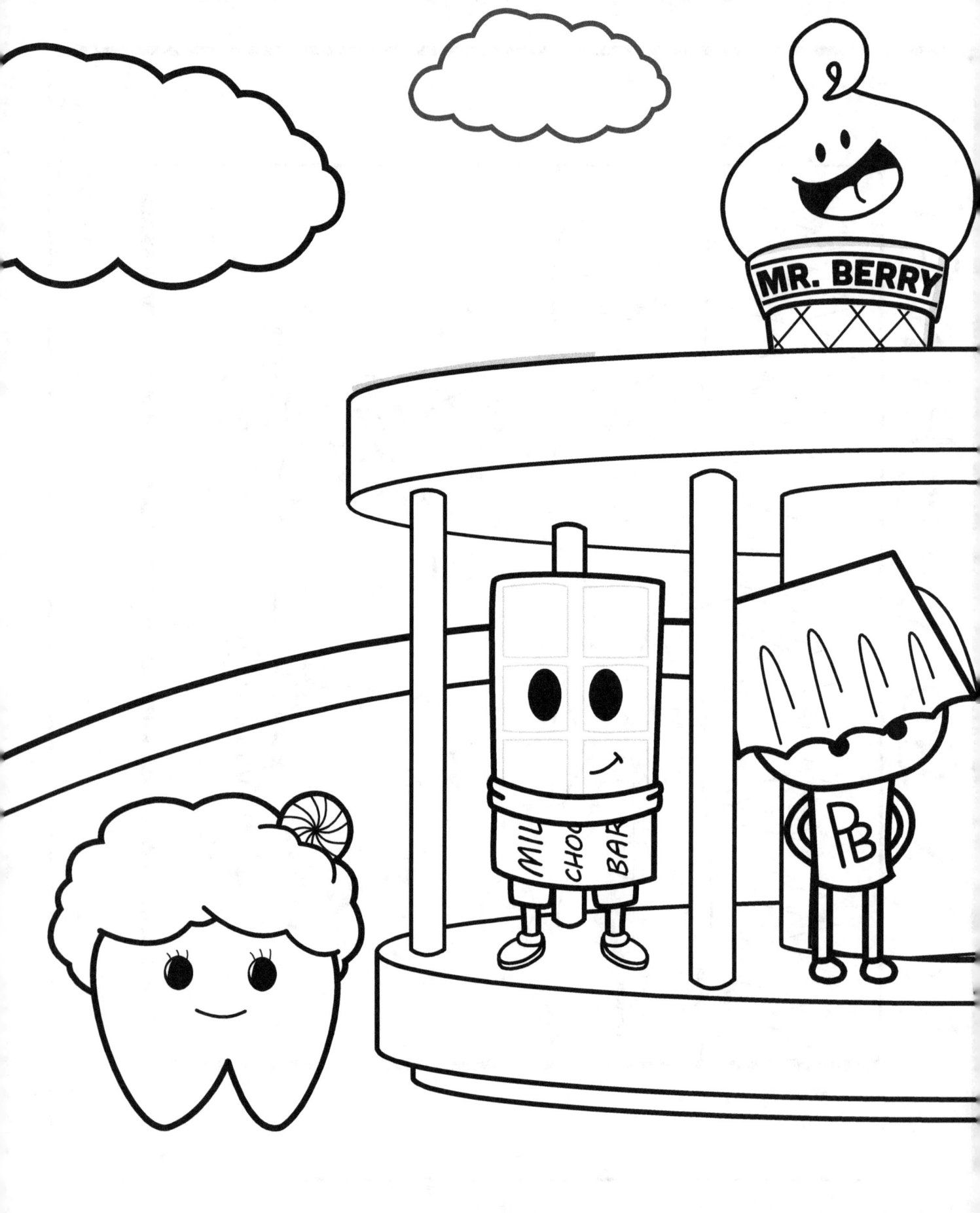

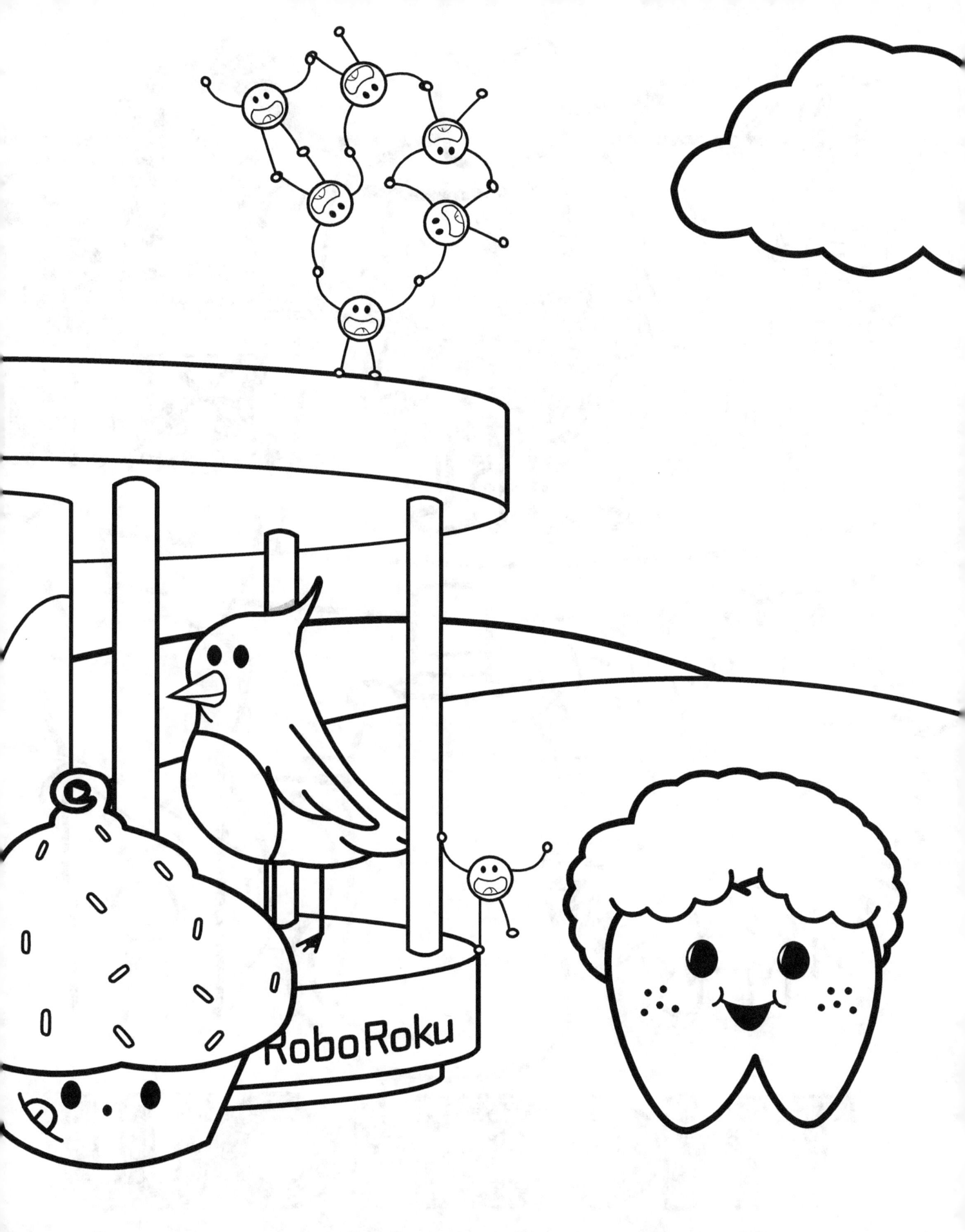

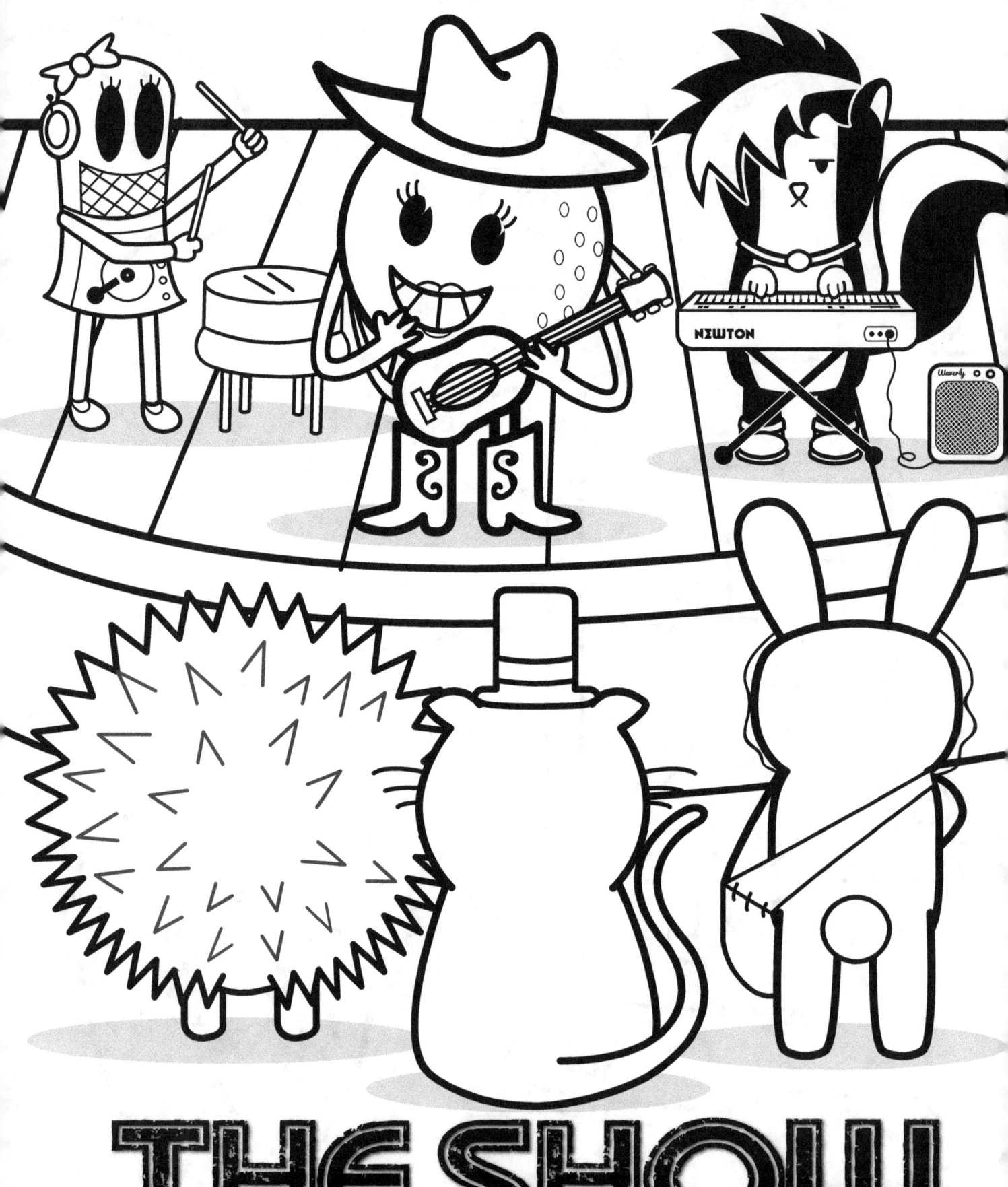

THE SHOW

Robo and Roku love to play music for their friends. Let's see who came to the show!

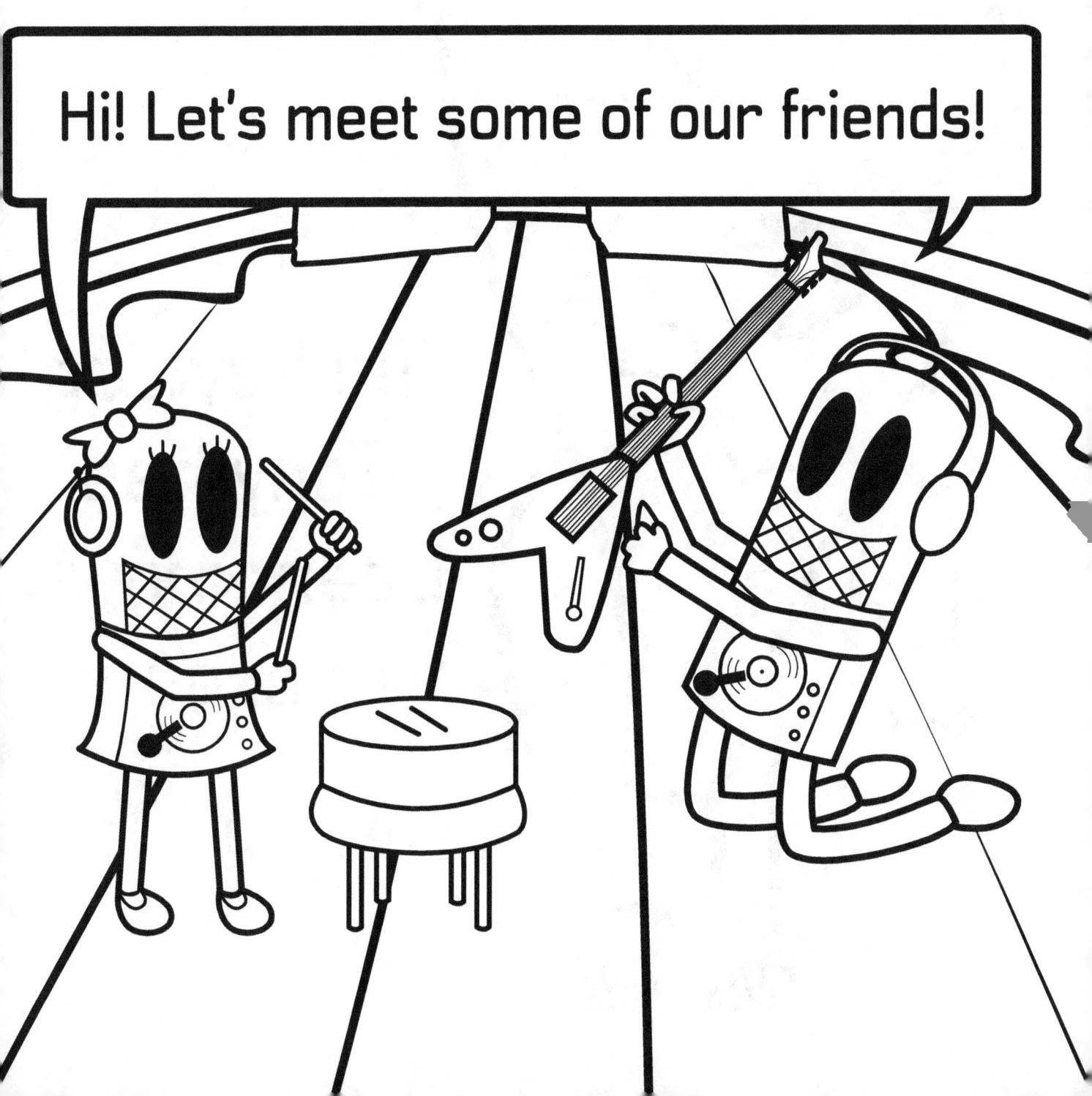

Hi! Let's meet some of our friends!

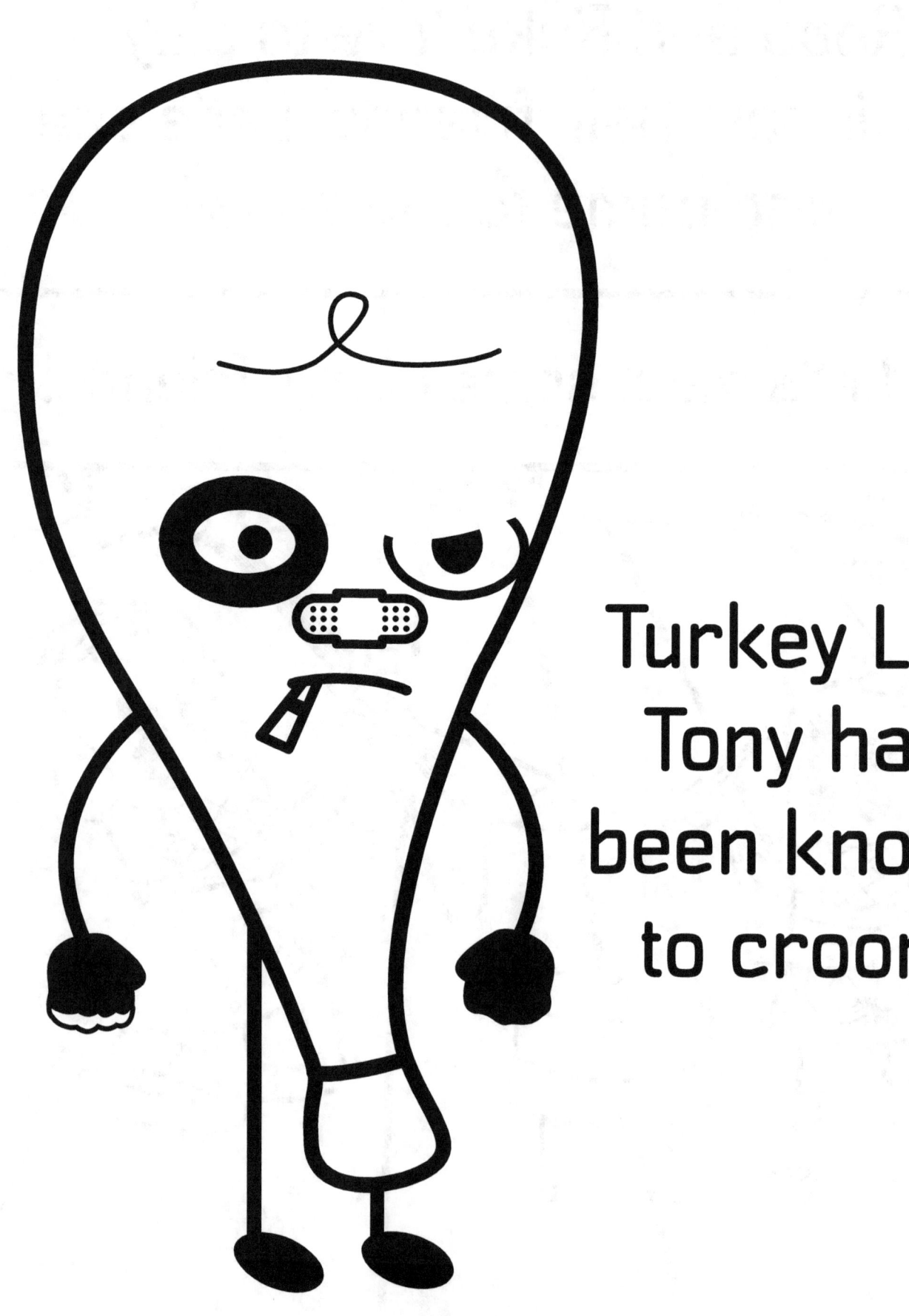

Turkey Leg
Tony has
been known
to croon.

Hard Hat
Harry loves
a nice loud
tune.

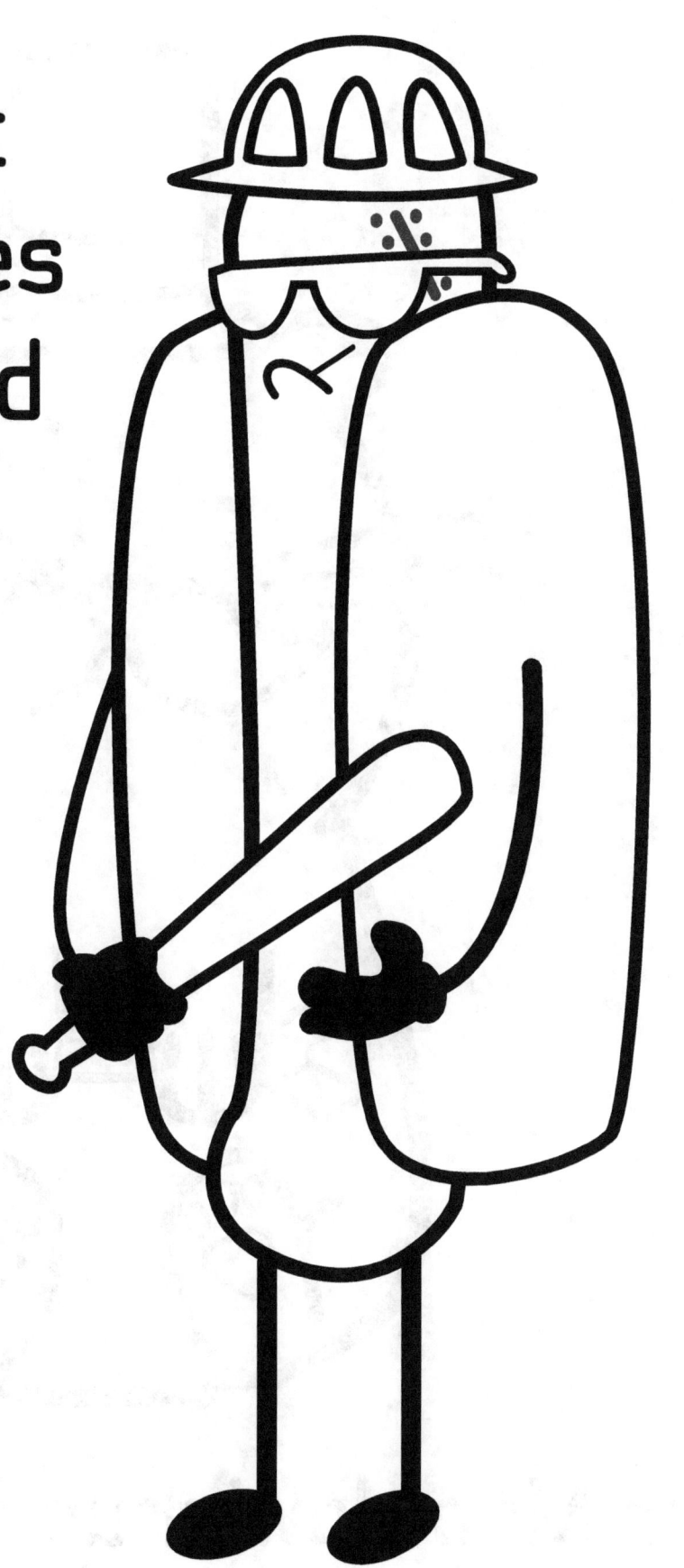

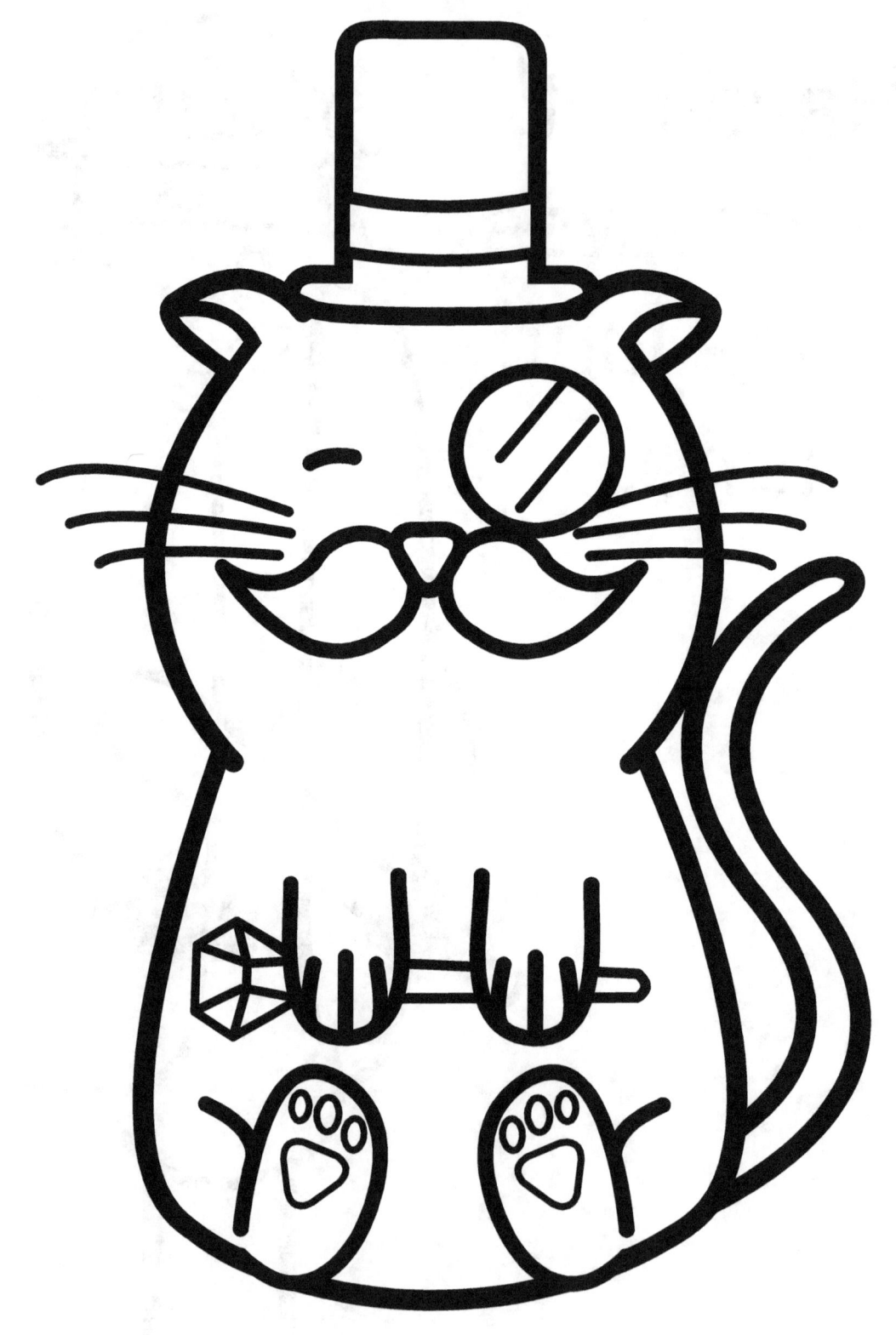

Sir Meowlowishus is a fancy cat!

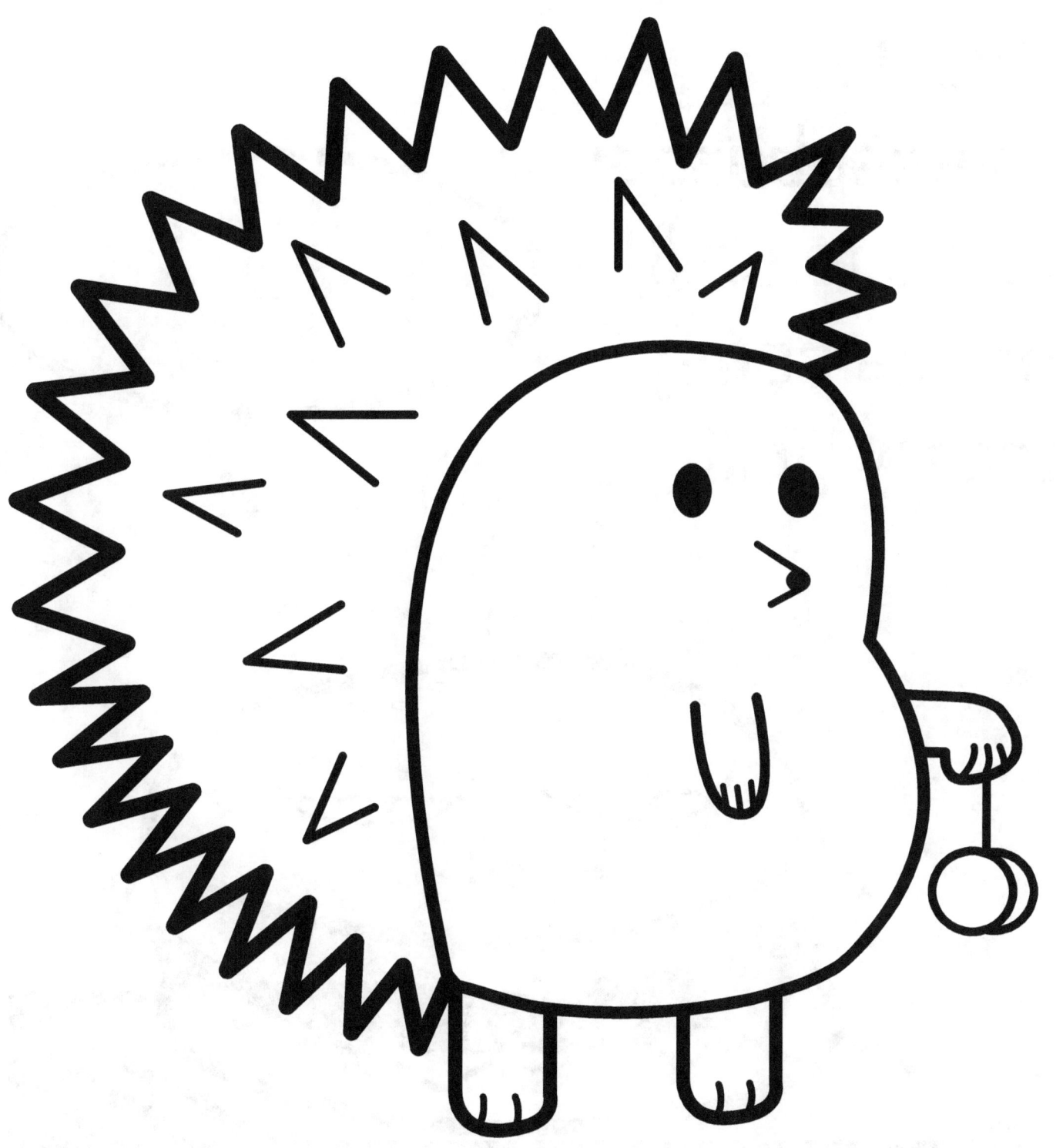

Duncan is a yo-yo champ.

Chester Cheeseburger loves to chill, on his comfy, toasty grill.

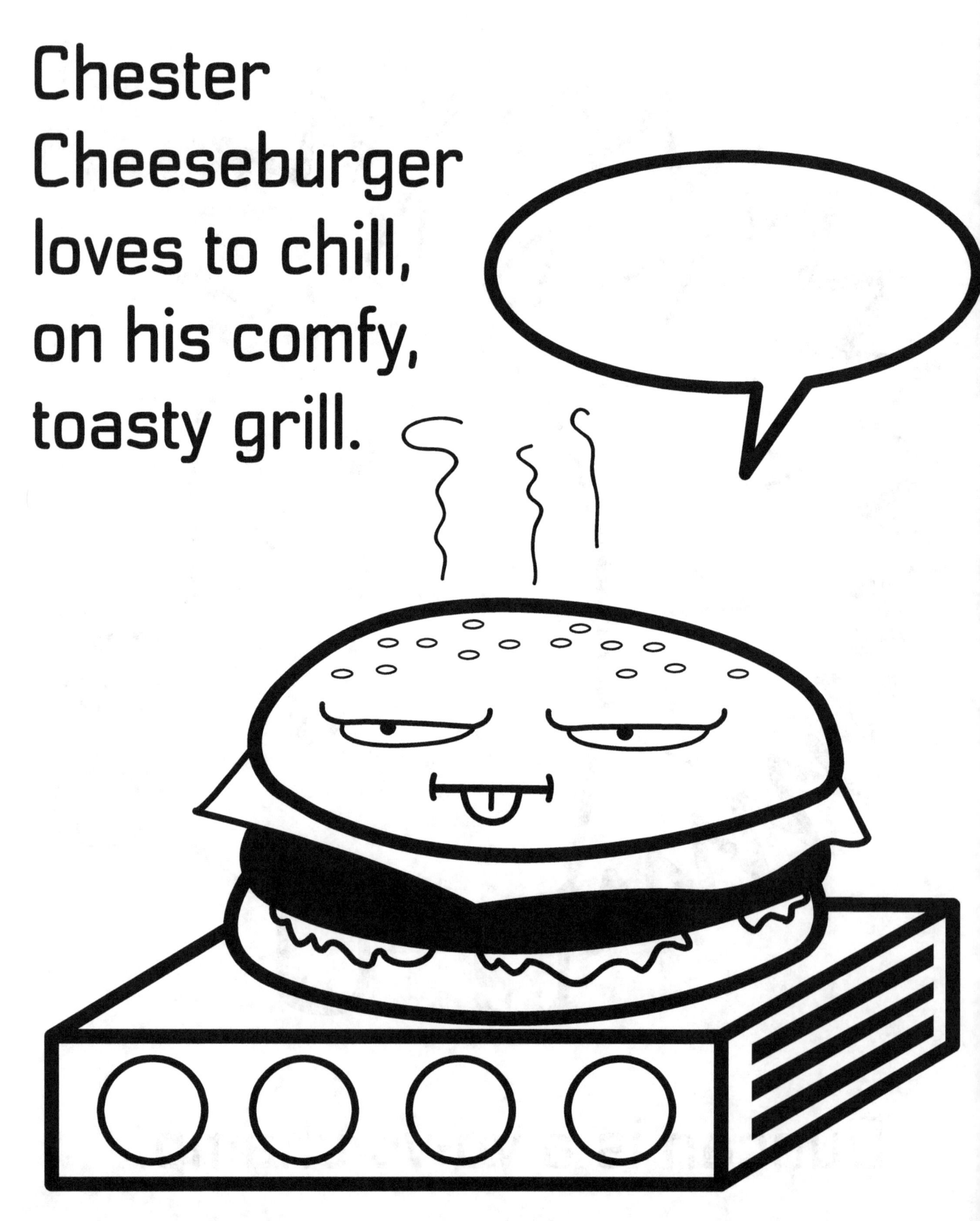

Rad Panda skated to the show in 6 seconds flat.

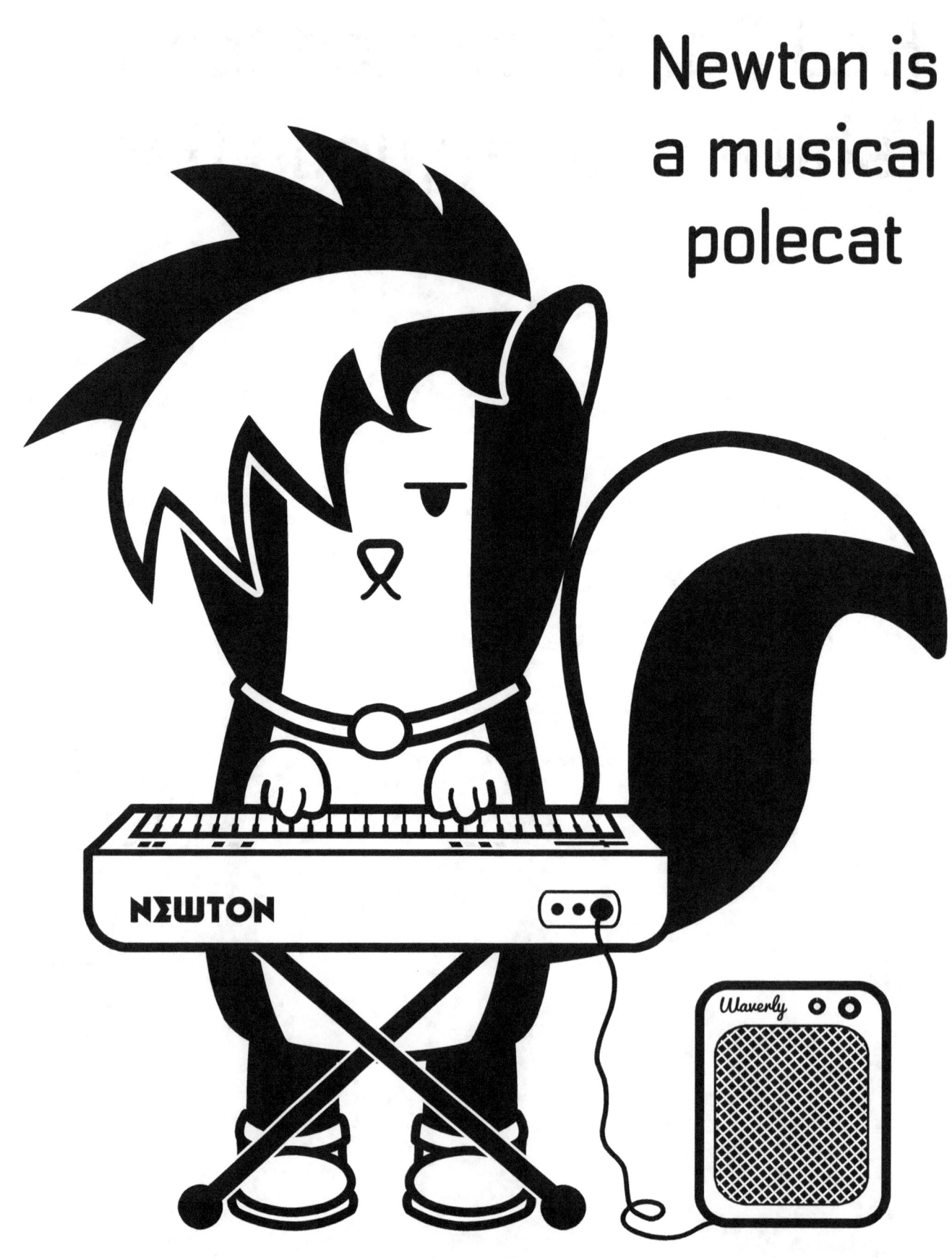

Newton is
a musical
polecat

And last but not least,
the band wouldn't play,
without Country Clementine
strumming away!

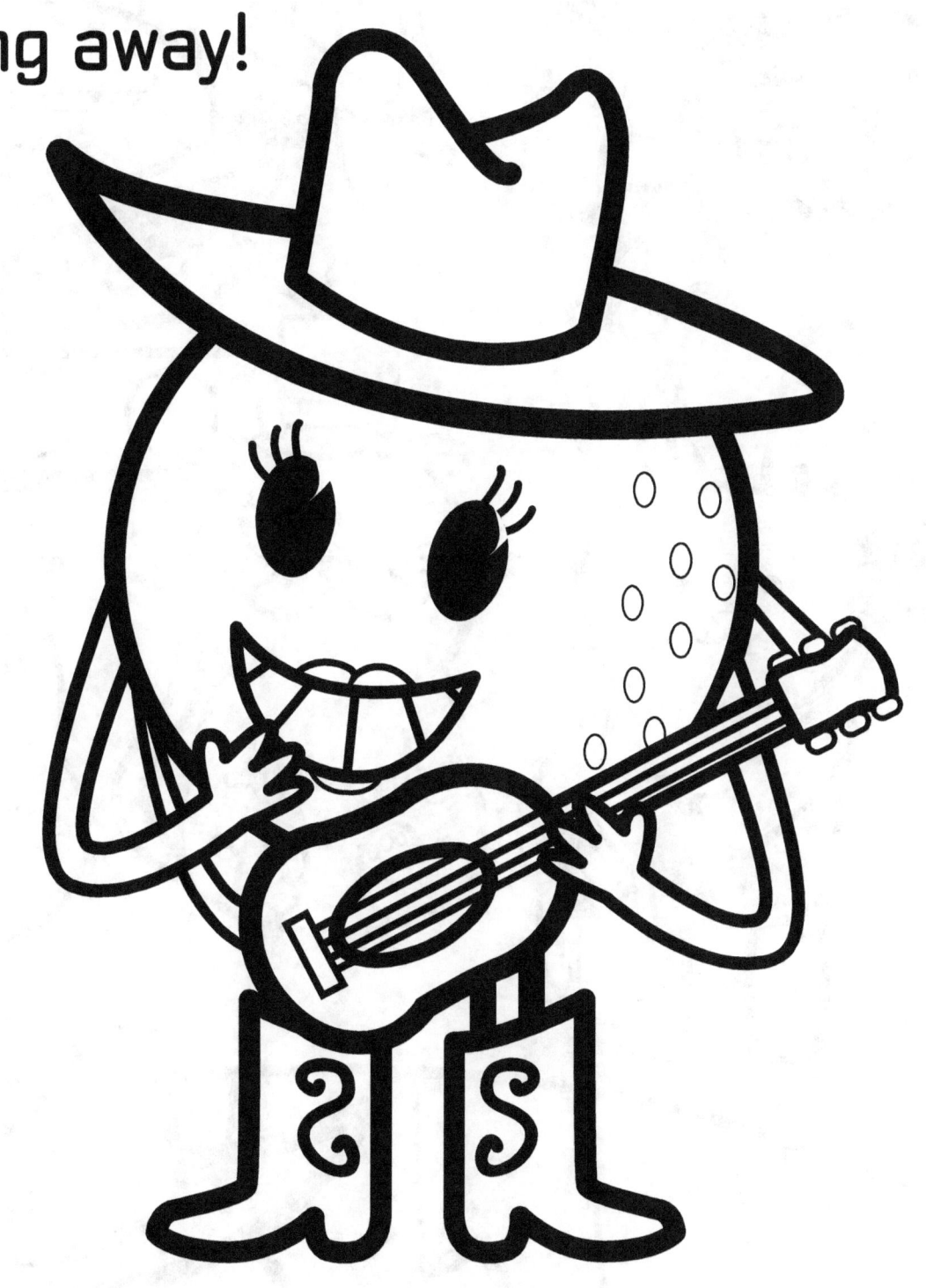

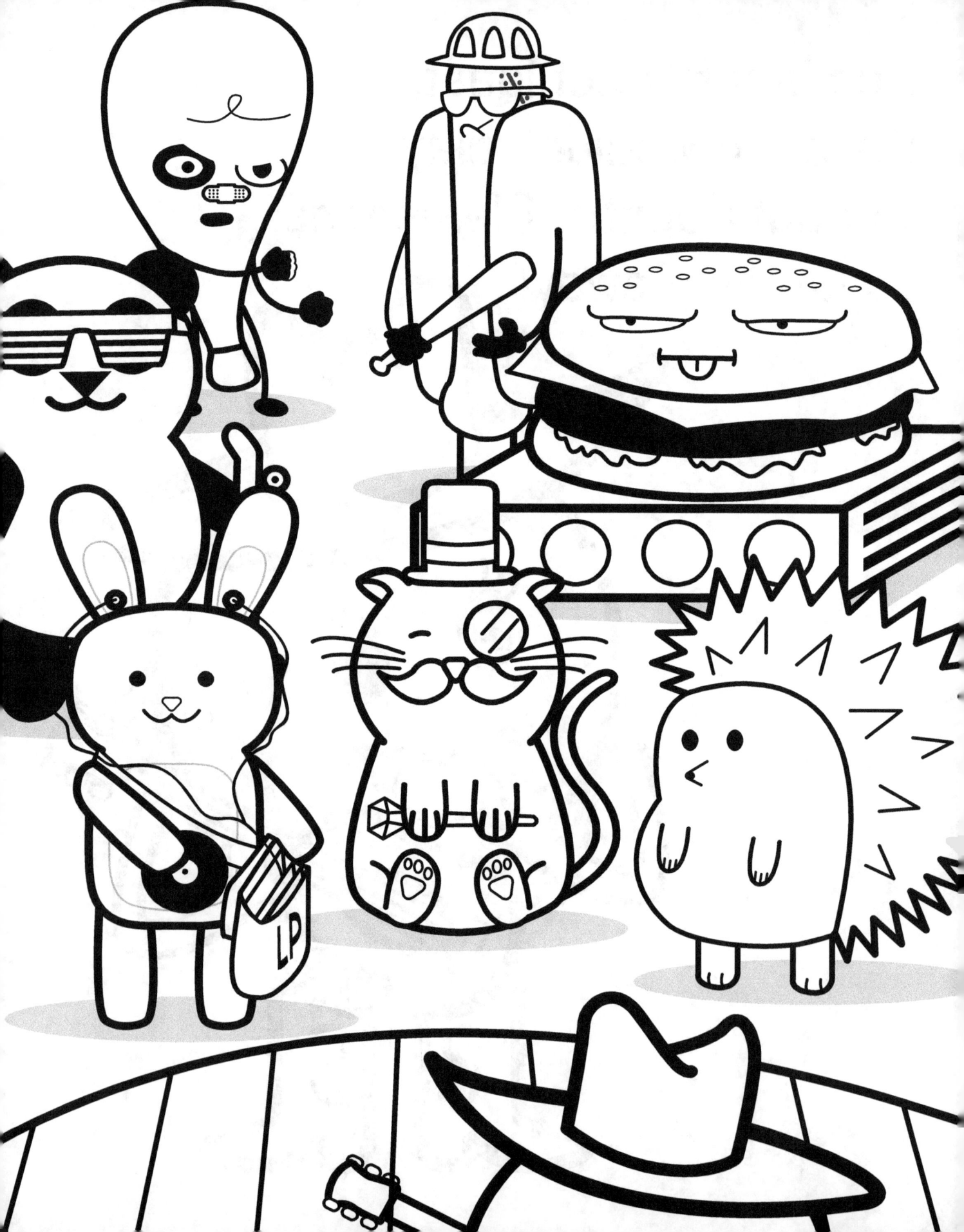

Blustery Boy

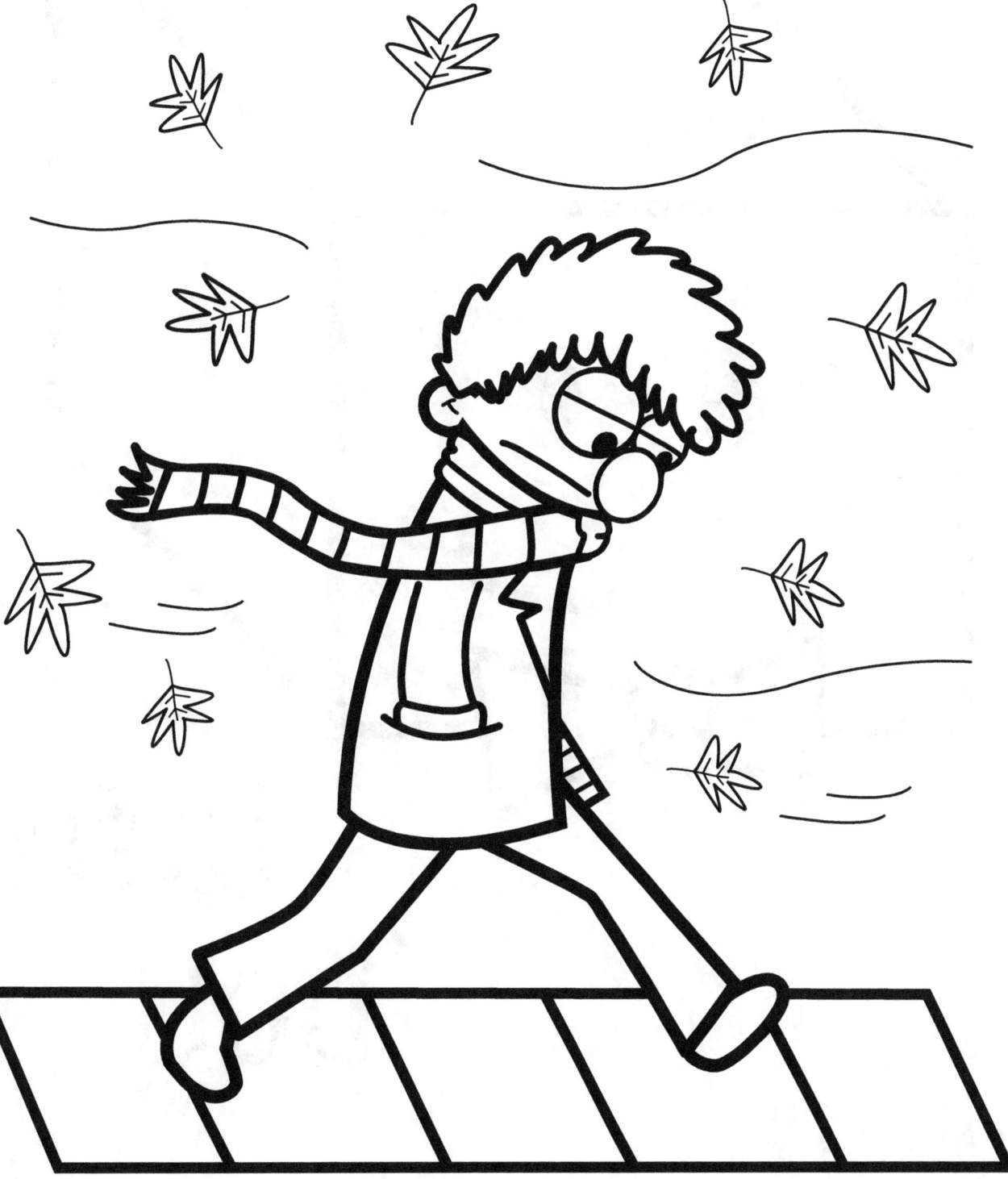

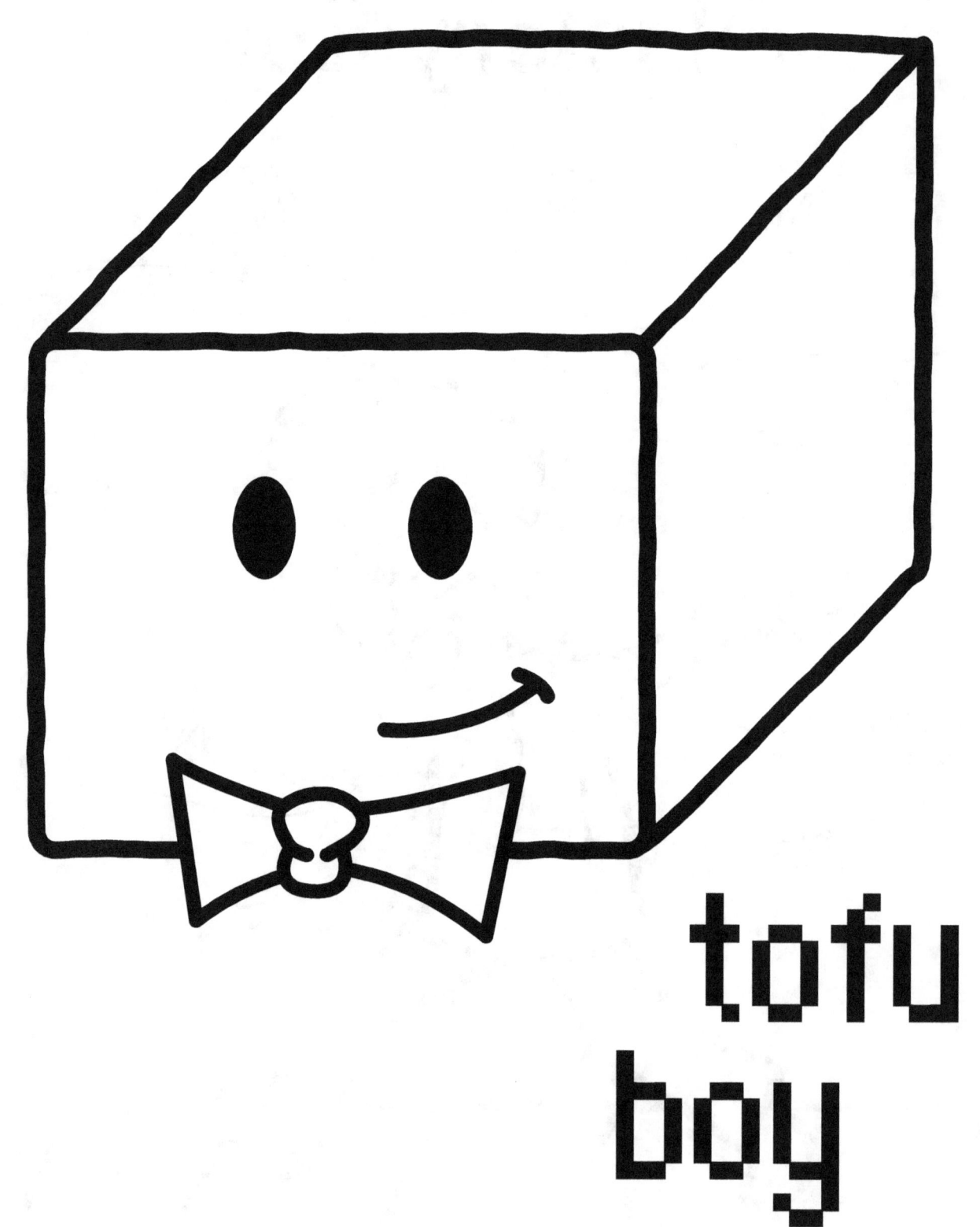

tofu
boy

tofu
girl

Make your own tofu!

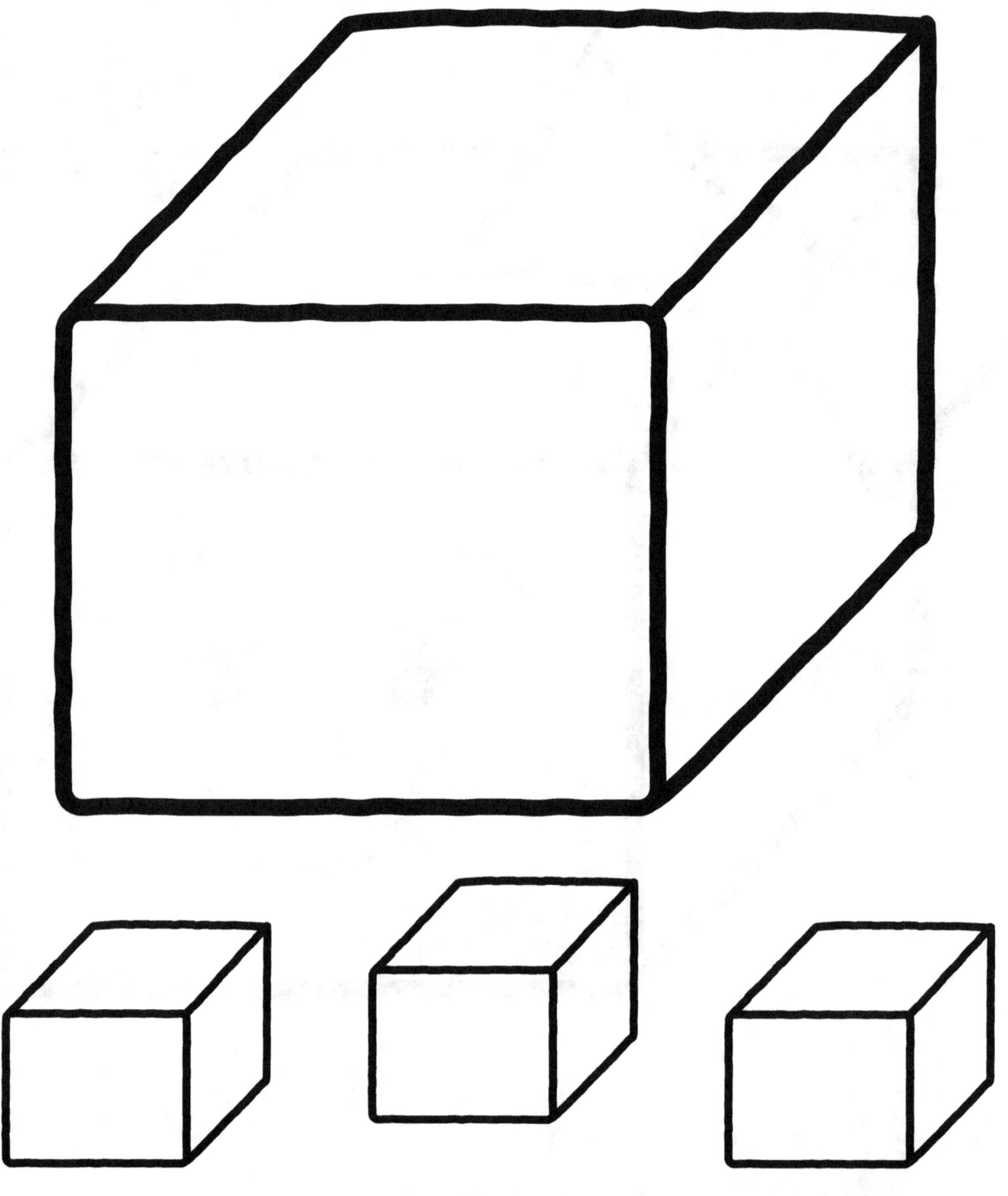

name
the books
he is
carrying!

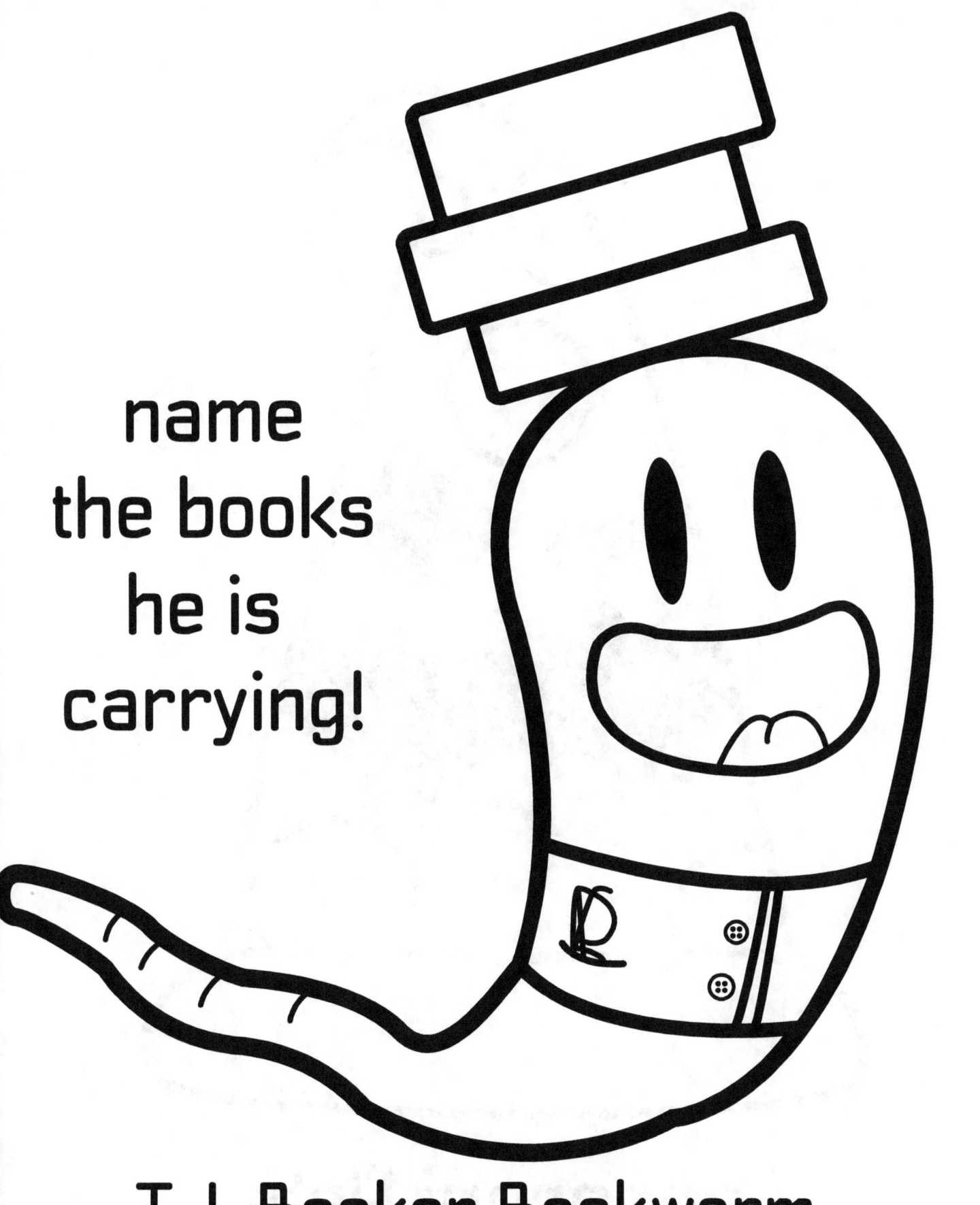

T.J. Booker Bookworm

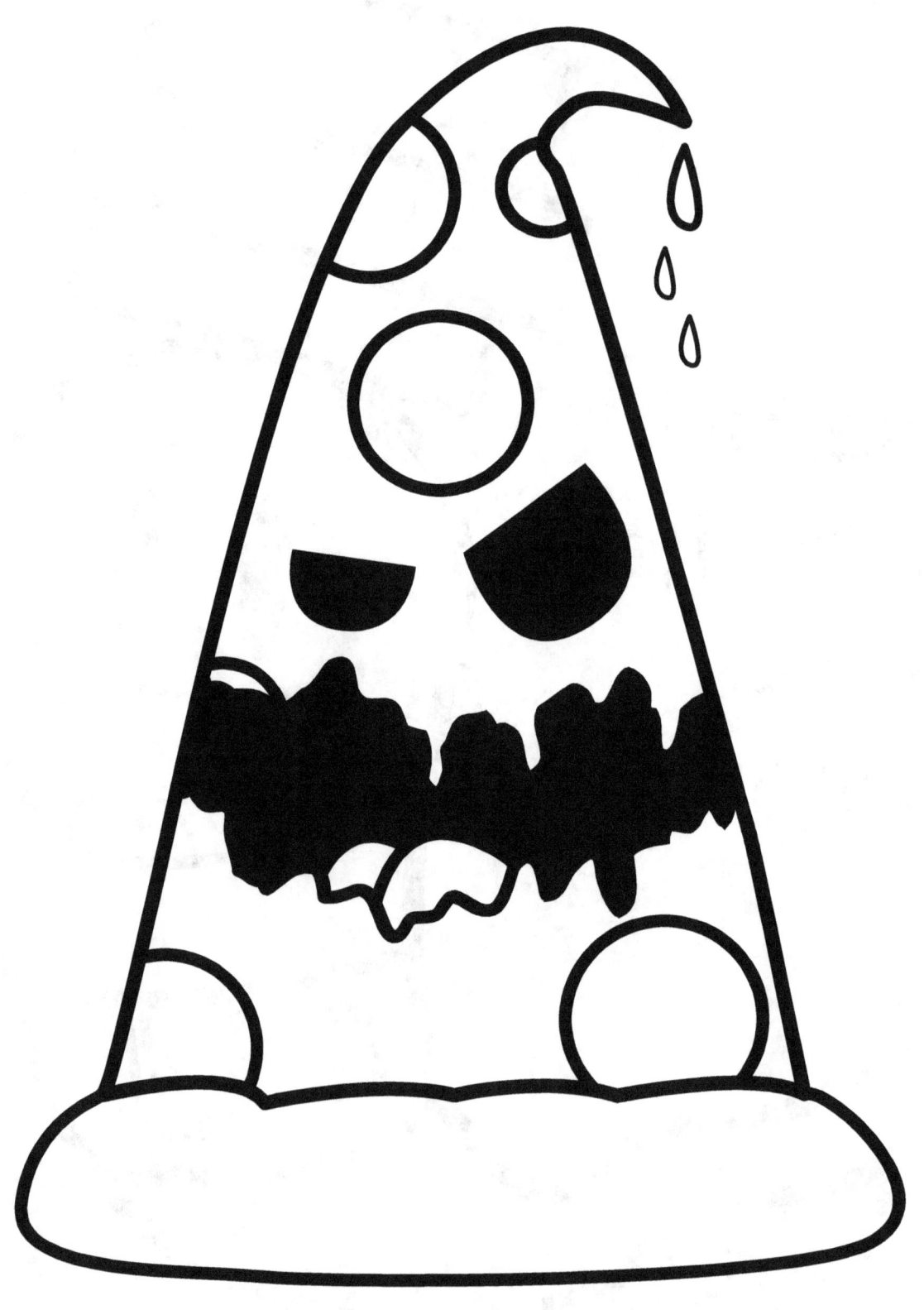

Pepperoni Pete

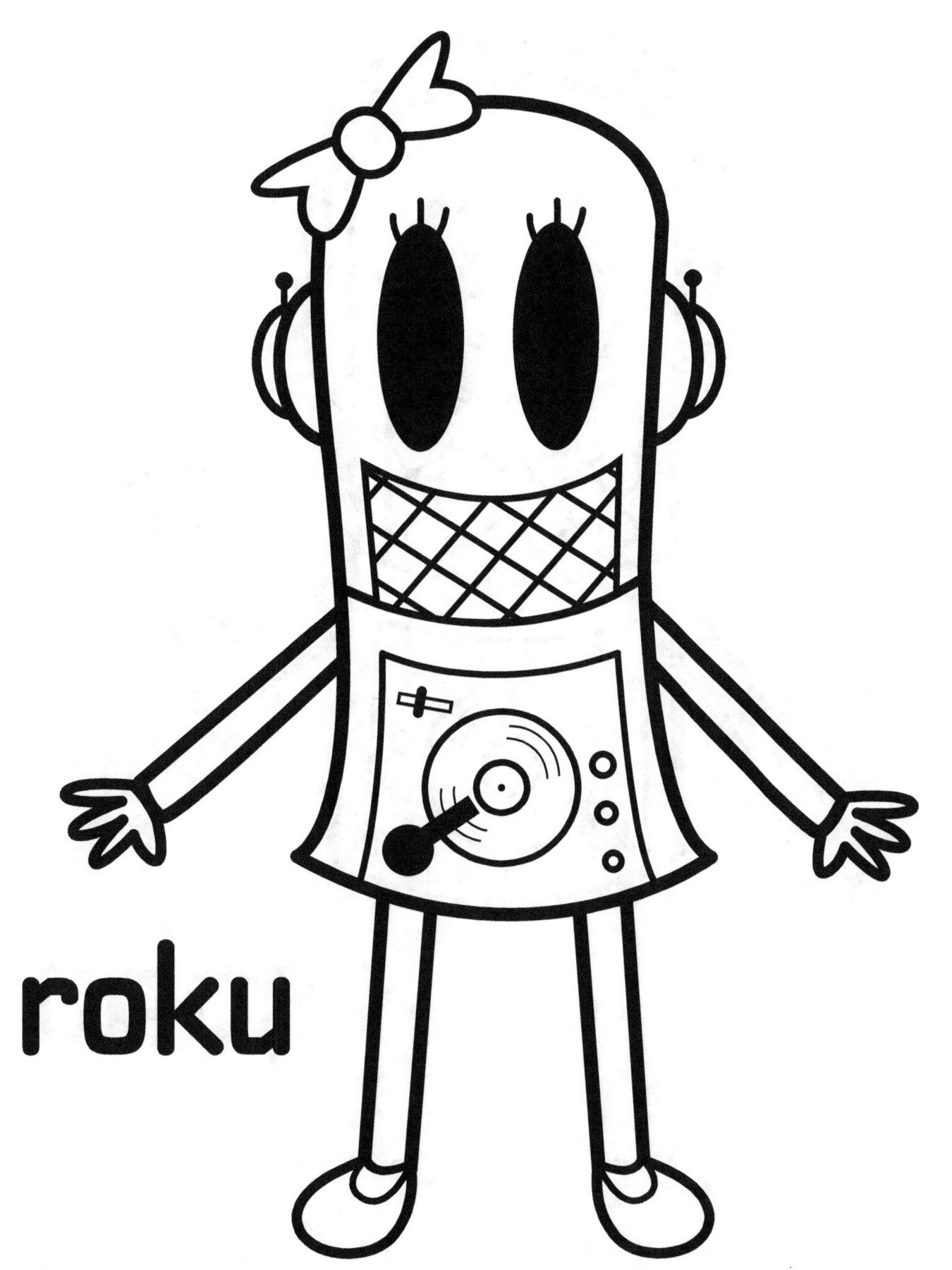

roku

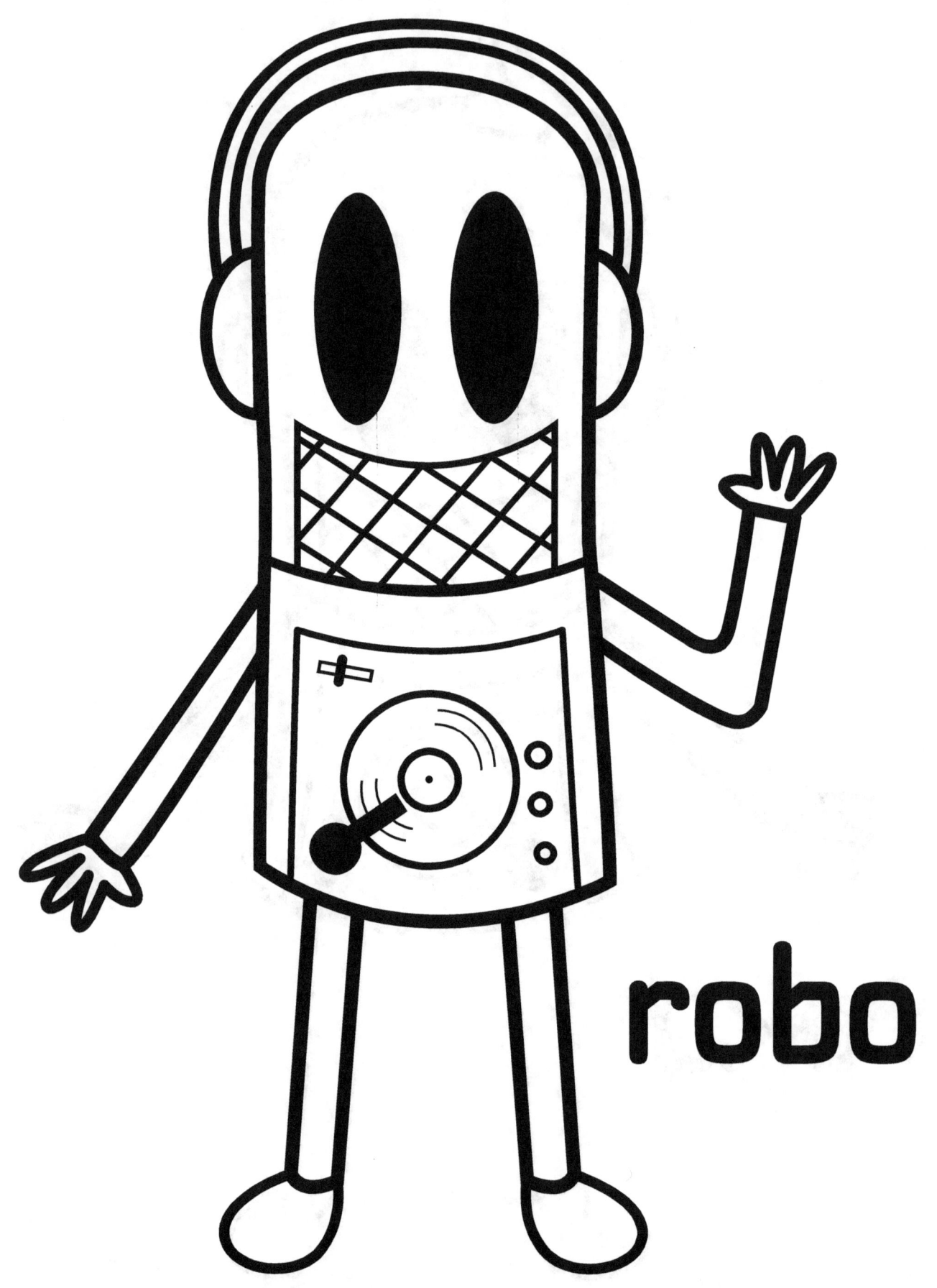

robo

Apple Jack

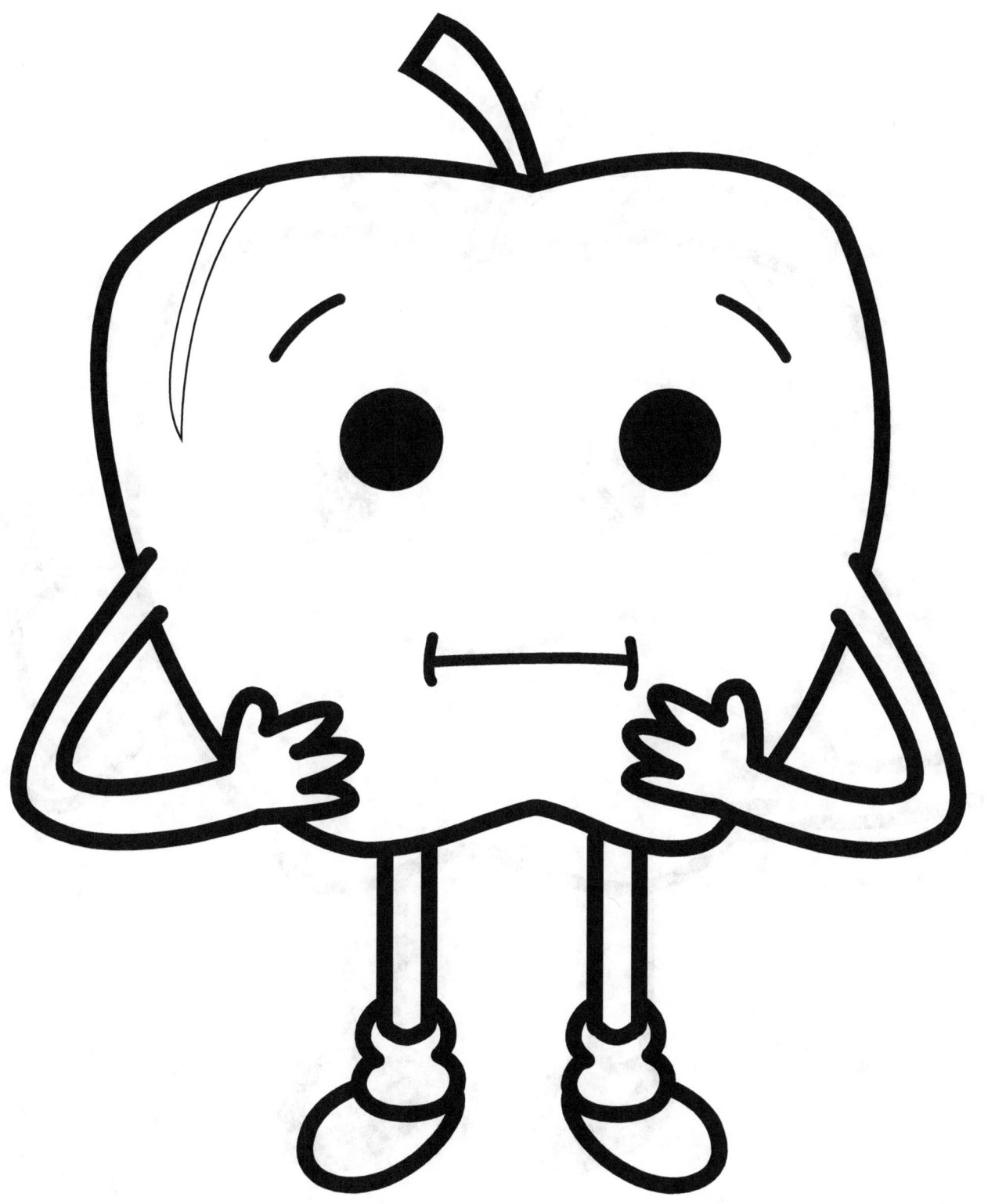

Apple Jill

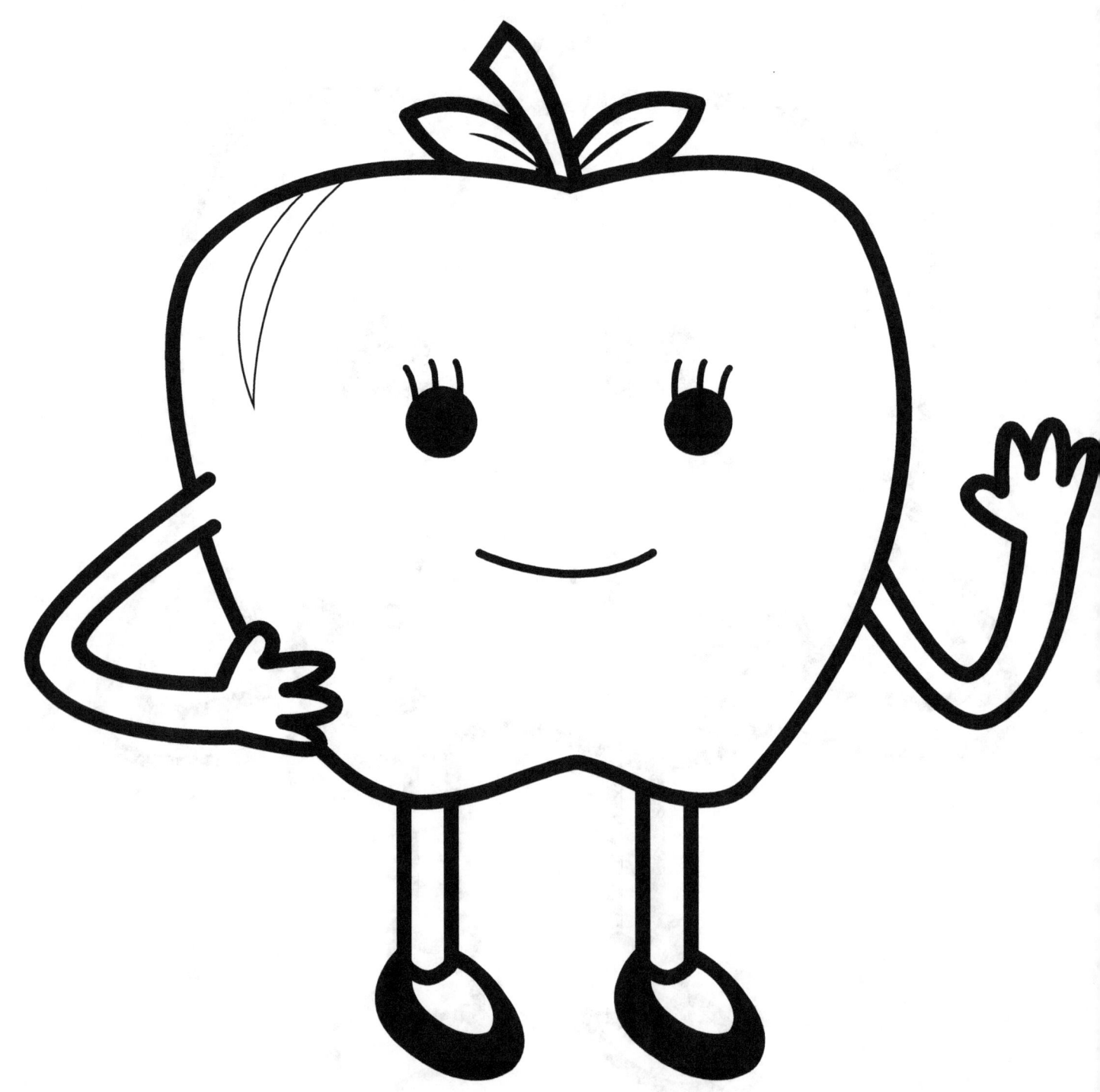

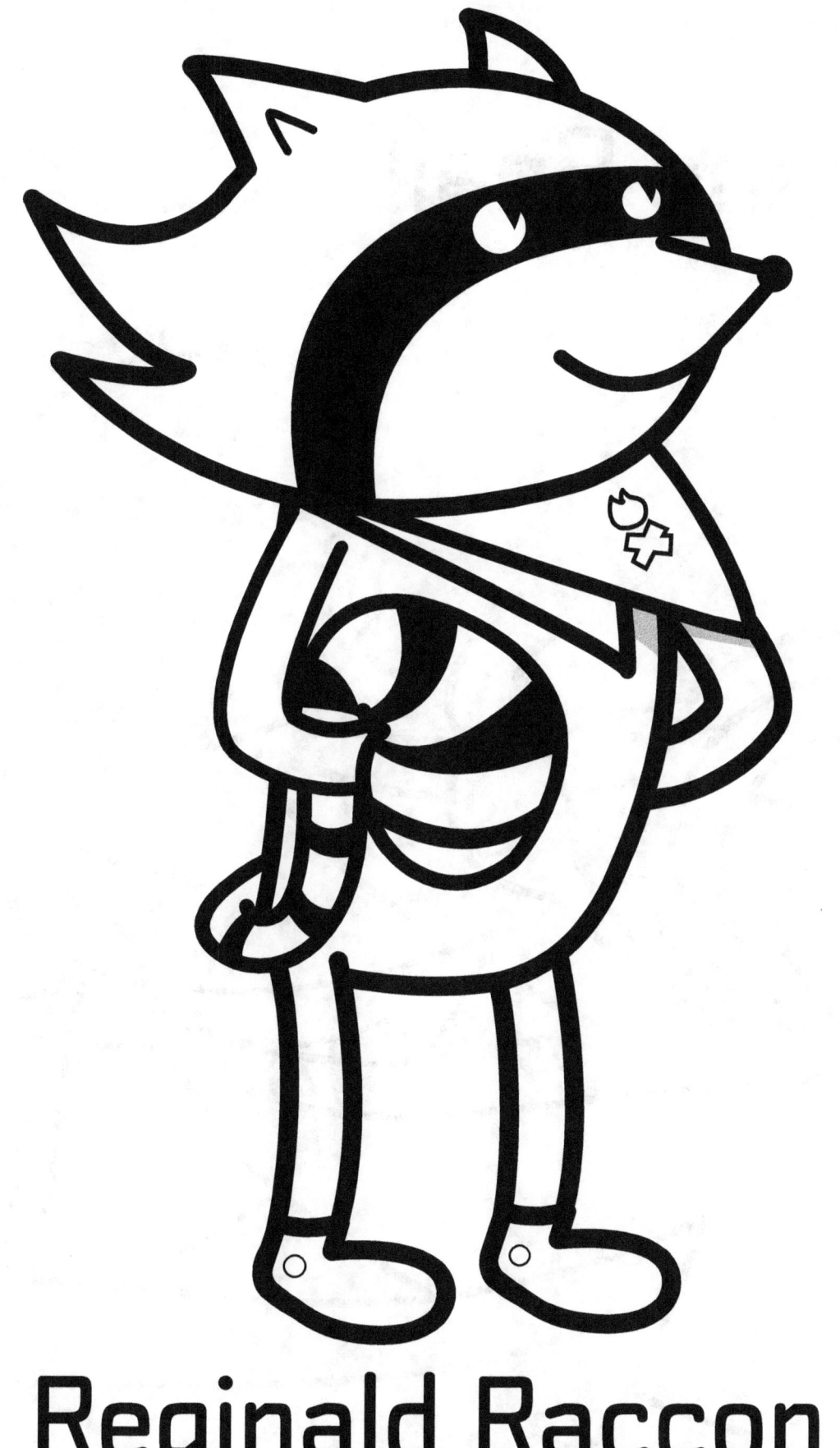

Reginald Raccon

Sy the Snail

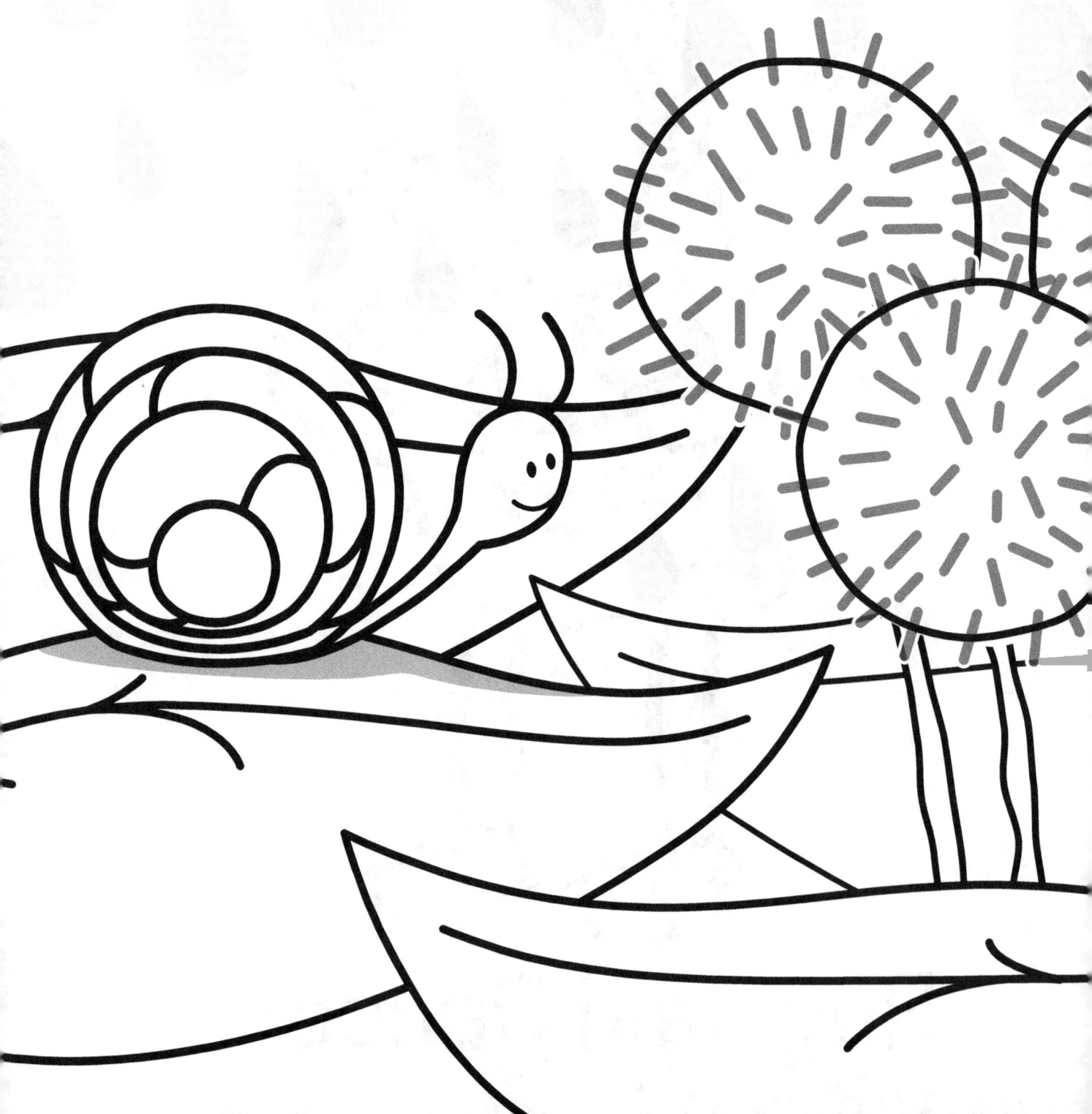

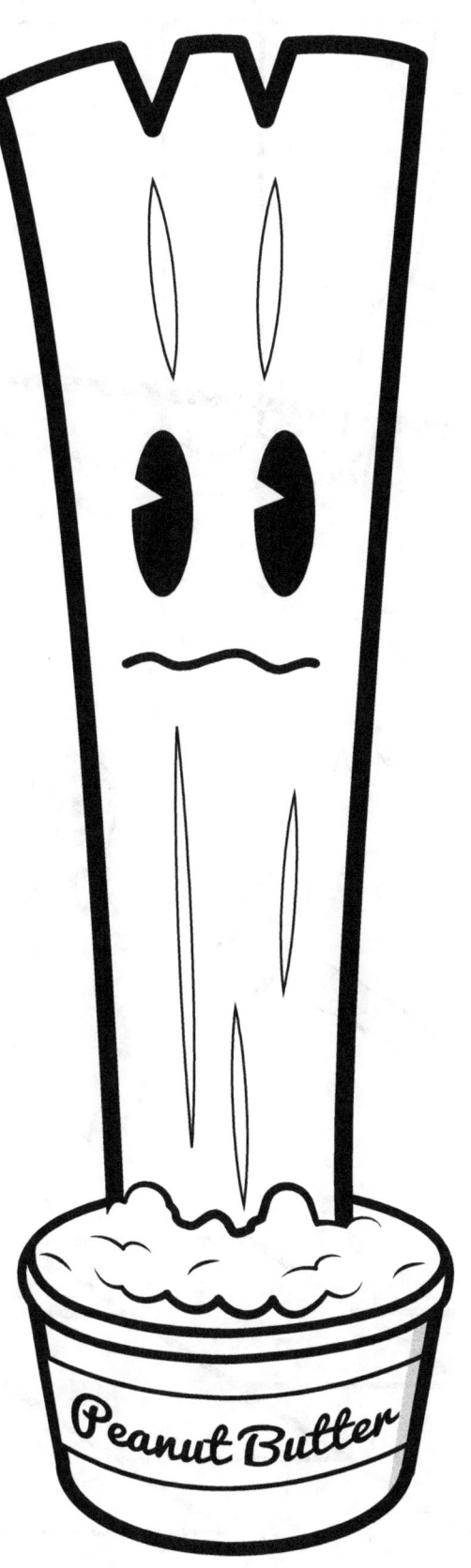

Cid
Celery

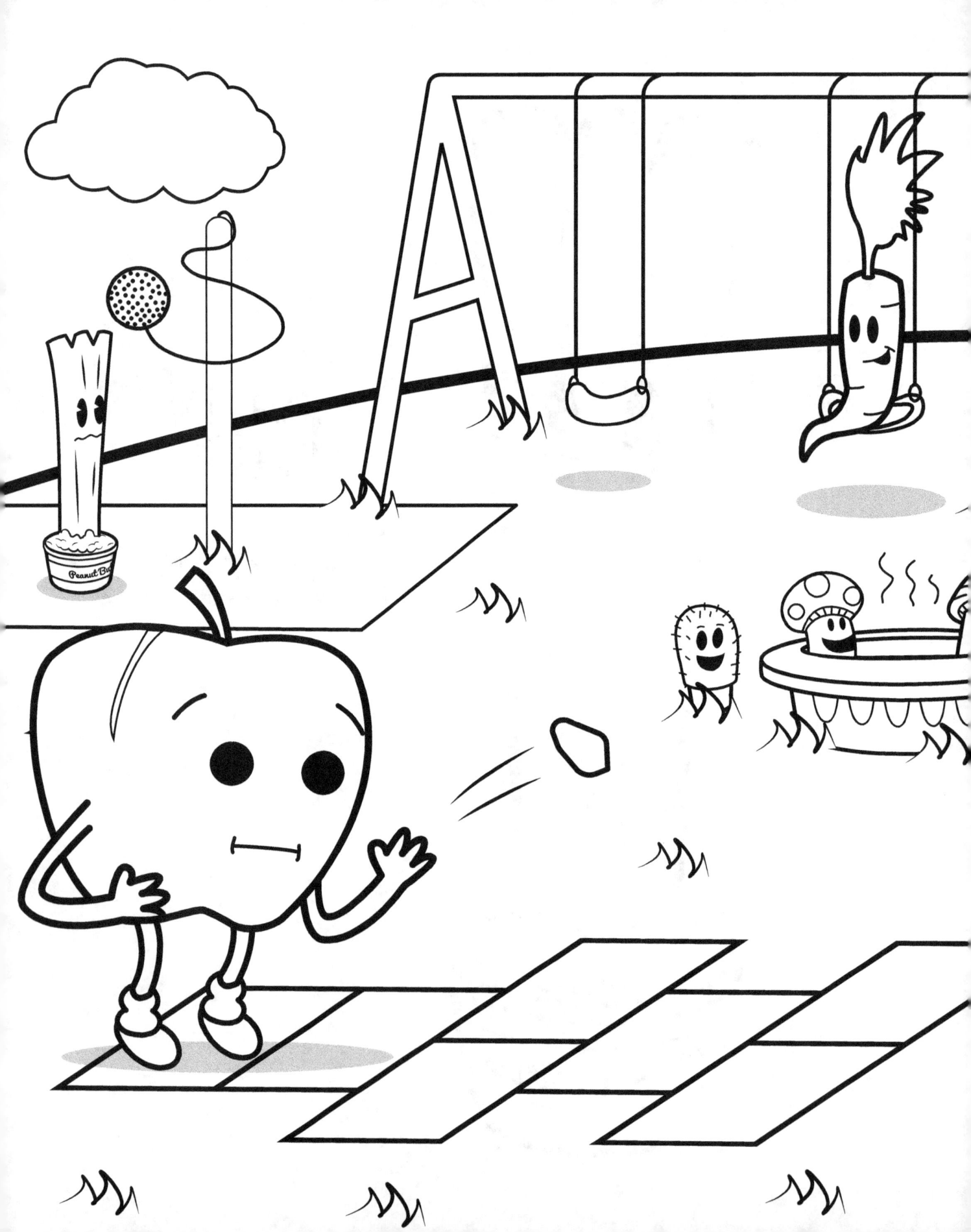

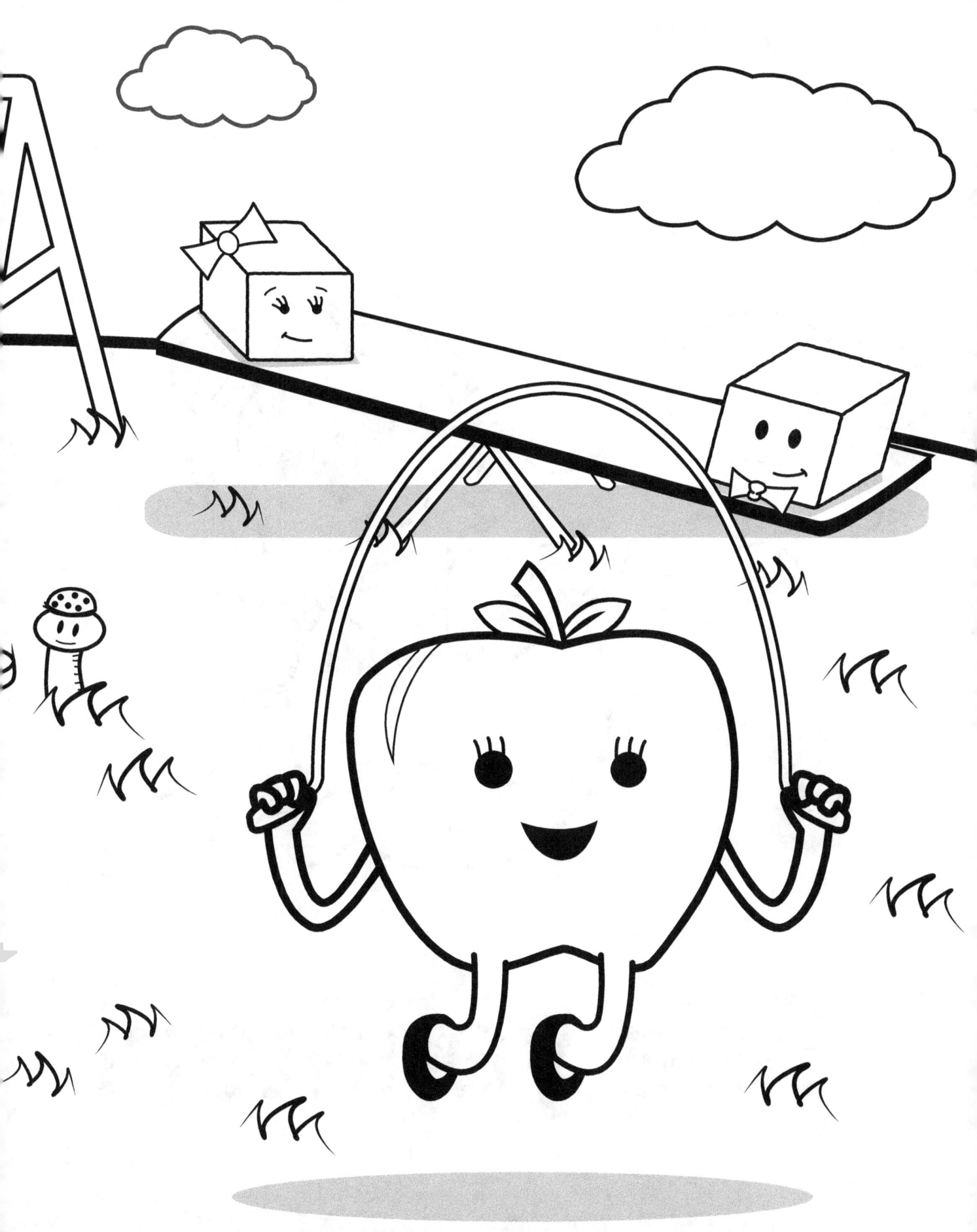

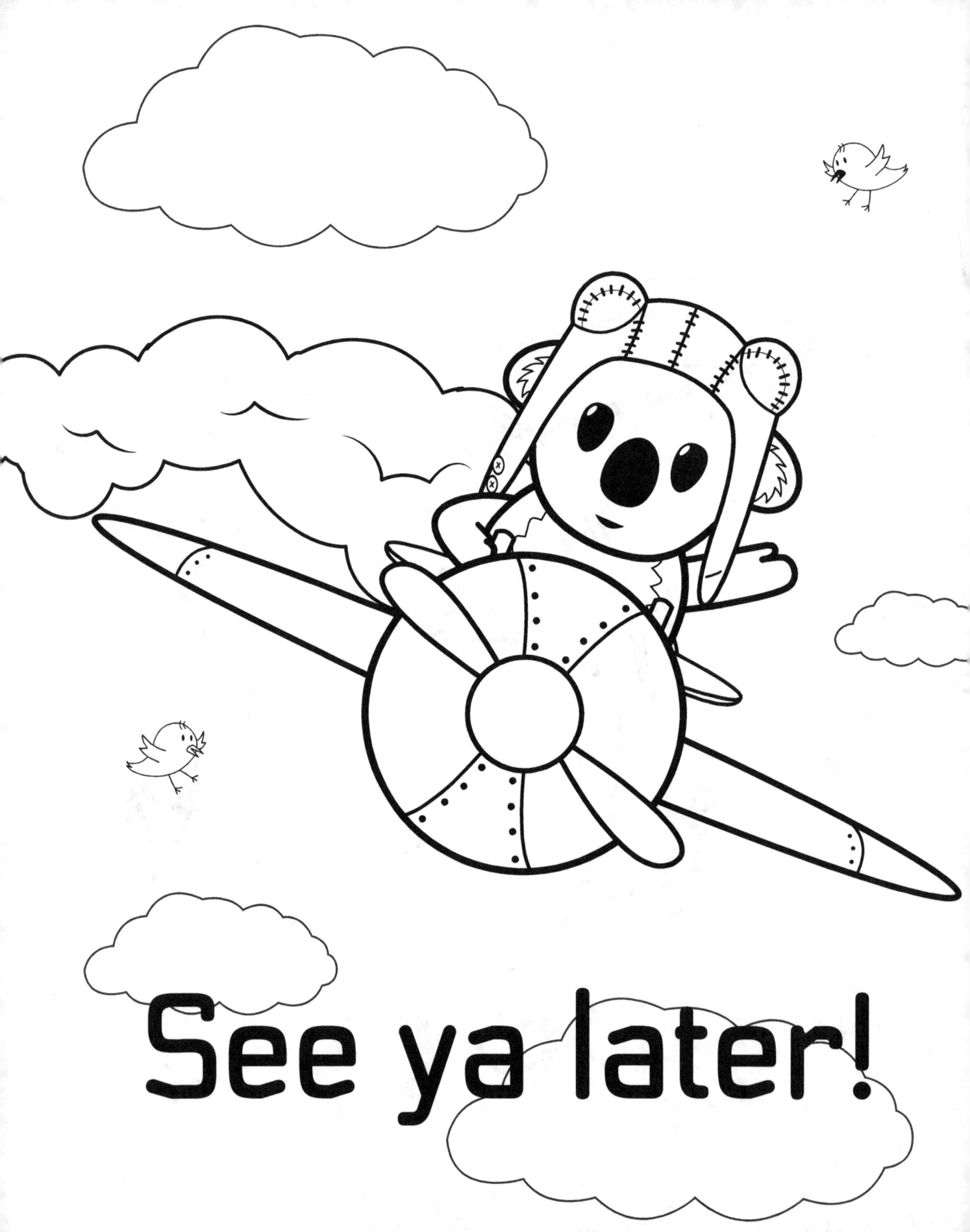

See ya later!

www.ingramcontent.com/pod-product-compliance
Lightning Source LLC
Chambersburg PA
CBHW080852170526
45158CB00009B/2716